I0755871

buildit

buildit

BUILDING BLINKIT IN AN EVOLVING INDIA

Albinder Singh Dhindsa

HARPER
BUSINESS

An Imprint of HarperCollins *Publishers*

First published in India by Harper Business 2026
An imprint of HarperCollins *Publishers*
HarperCollins *Publishers* India, Cyber City,
Building 10-A, Gurugram, Haryana – 122002, India
www.harpercollins.co.in

2 4 6 8 10 9 7 5 3 1

P-ISBN: 978-93-6989-943-2
E-ISBN: 978-93-6989-389-8

Typeset in 11.5/15.2 Adobe Caslon Pro
by HarperCollins *Publishers* India Pvt. Ltd

HarperCollins *Publishers*, Macken House, 39/40 Mayor Street Upper,
Dublin 1, D01 C9W8, Ireland

CONTENTS

A JOURNEY OF TWO DECADES

2004

I left Punjab for Delhi on 8 August 2000 for a college education. Exactly four years later, to the day, I was on the move again. This time, I left Delhi for the United States of America and landed among the vibrant and industrious student community in Orlando, Florida—barely three months after my last set of classes in college.

My first week in Florida was an introduction to American ingenuity and abundance, to the country's effectiveness and its congruence. It also led to a very vivid realization of what managing chaos in an unpredictable world looked like. Years earlier, as a child growing up in Patiala, I remember peeping out through the windows of my home and witnessing the ravages of floods in my city. The rising waters brought about real tragedy—the loss of homes, loved ones and livelihood. The horrific stories and menacing dark clouds instilled in me a fear of losing those close to me and an almost fatalistic acceptance of my powerlessness against raging nature.

Four days after I landed in Florida, my roommate Nezam, a senior from college, and I sat next to the window of our small two-bedroom apartment, looking at uprooted trees on the street outside as winds of 250 km/hr battered the city. Hurricane Charley had struck Orlando that evening. There was an evacuation order in effect, but we did not know anyone in town yet, so we had nowhere to go. We were fearful and helpless. We just sat and watched as the hurricane winds took off the roofs of houses and power lines collapsed into the marshes between the apartment complexes. As the winds subsided by early morning, the government swung into action to clean up the debris and fix the heavy power lines that had gone down; within 48 hours power was restored like nothing had happened. Perhaps we were not that helpless after all.

Nezam and I survived those two days of shutdown and power outage drinking milk that was rapidly curdling and consuming sugary donuts. We were getting desperate as we waited—soon we would have to resort to eating raw eggs and whatever uncooked stuff we had in the fridge. It did not come down to that, though. Even though the hurricane had done much damage, the system had moved efficiently, its swift and effective response ensuring that essential services became accessible very quickly, and we marvelled at how the First World functioned. We only had to live without power for two days and that too in a temperate climate—this felt easier than experiencing power cuts in the brutal heat of Delhi during college over the previous four years. We really thought America had it all figured out. Even today, when I see systemic responses in India, whether state-led or driven by private organizations, fail to deliver on their actual intentions, I feel a pinch of remorse followed by hope that it is possible to survive such collapses.

The handling of the aftermath of Hurricane Charley was proof that things worked differently in America than they did in India. As a twenty-two-year-old with no ideology or orientation, I was discovering new things and marvelling at the efficiency of the country I had just landed in.

On my second day in Orlando, the university's support desk for foreign students had recommended that new students buy whatever they needed on Amazon.com. They said it was a website that sold innumerable products that would be delivered as early as the very next day. To me, this was unbelievable, and I was fascinated by yet another example of American enterprise. There were millions of products that could just appear at my doorstep within a day—all I had to do was click a few buttons on my laptop.

I spent the first few nights after I got access to the internet scanning the different and random products that I could buy on Amazon, gaping at the incredible prices. I flipped webpage after webpage of the world's largest catalogue of products. When the power lines had gone down during the hurricane, apart from hot meals, the only thing I missed was being suddenly cut off from this amazing website that had the coolest things I had never thought of buying. Even before my first scholarship cheque hit my bank account, I had made a list of items that I thought I absolutely needed to buy. The day I got access to the first scholarship deposit of $330, I spent almost a third of it on Amazon. I remember buying a wireless mouse, an onion cutter, a book on machine learning and a small USB tool. In fact, even today, all these purchases reflect on my Amazon US account. Suddenly, it felt like I had accessed a portal that empowered me to solve all my problems in life. A part for a broken faucet, a new kettle, a cheaper version of a textbook—everything was just a few clicks away, and I was hooked. I was unaware at the time that this obsession with Amazon would reflect in my entrepreneurial choices years later.

One of the first products I ordered, though, turned out to be faulty. It was a USB adapter to connect the computer to Wi-Fi. In those days, most desktops and laptops could only connect to the internet through a LAN cable and ethernet port. But here was this device that could convert my cheap laptop, bought from Nehru Place in Delhi, into a modern machine which could connect to the internet over the air, making it truly portable. The only problem was that the device I had bought didn't work. I dutifully informed Amazon and they sent someone to pick it up the next day. Meanwhile, I discovered that the seller of the product was someone in Missouri, a midwestern state in America.

The seller pinged me to ask what problems I was facing with the device. As we chatted over Amazon's review system, it struck me that this person and Amazon, the company, were located in different parts of the country. Amazon was based out of Seattle, Washington, and the seller was operating from St. Louis, Missouri—two different parts of the country, geographically, ideologically and even culturally very far apart. Except that the two worlds were cooperating to deliver to me a bit of hardware that would fill me with joy every once in a while, mostly watching memes on the internet, when I didn't want the bother of being tethered to a wire.

In my first brush with the American way of life, Amazon gave me a peek into its world of commerce and capitalism. As a society we might not agree on a lot of things, but we cooperate and are connected through the activity of commerce. It is a silent, necessary part of life that compels humanity to acknowledge that we really do need each other to survive and thrive, no matter the boundaries we have set up for ourselves—whether along religious, cultural, caste, national or ideological lines. The laptop I am using to write this book might have been made by people with whom I have no shared sense of identity; they probably stand for a point of view that is the polar opposite of mine, but commerce is making me transact with them, and this act of cooperation, despite the burden of differences, is what allows for innovation and progress.

Amazon redefined how commerce could be conducted in today's social environment, at a scale of impact probably not experienced since the Silk Road reshaped global trade. It would be years later, after my first experience of it, that I would fully process the moment when I started feeling a tug towards the act of buying and selling products and my love for commerce. As amazed and smitten as I was at the time with this accessible website that had an infinite catalogue, I soon discovered another company that got people across continents to collaborate for even apparently trivial things.

The first time I set foot in a Walmart was a life-changing experience. Every item was priced way below my expectations. Despite going from a country like India, the range of their products and prices looked too good to be true. How was a pack of six T-shirts available for $4.99 (about ₹250 at the time)? Nezam and I pretty much spent our entire stipends on things we didn't know we needed. I remember buying so much frozen food only to realize when we got home that our fridge was not big enough to hold even half of it (forcing us to beg another student to store it in his fridge). And it was not just food. We were blown away by the number of household items and clothes we could buy for cheap. More amazingly, here was a company that was as American as it got, yet everything in the store said 'Made in China'.

In its search for efficiency and the lowest prices for customers, Sam Walton's company had created a commerce bridge between

America and China. A definitive two-way bridge which made their interdependency real and eternal—in the American economy people got access to affordable products and could pursue higher value enterprise, while the Chinese economy built itself on manufacturing for a vast market. From the elderly retirees who greeted you when you showed up at a Walmart store (a practice to encourage employment for older folks who still needed an income after their retirement) to the expansive selection of fishing rods in the back, it felt like Walmart had woven itself deeply into the social and economic fabric of the country. I felt a sense of awe at the meticulous way the company had built its business, by collaborating with people from a country with an entirely different value system. The contrast between what I knew and what I was learning every day was too sharp for me to forget easily.

From my early experiences of Amazon and Walmart, I formed a healthy curiosity for retail in general and an appreciation for the impact that these companies had on the quality of life of so many people in America. There was an almost instant urge to set up something similar in India—to change how things were bought and improve the quality of life of people in India, while seeking opportunity for myself. However, at the time, practical considerations meant that it was just a passing thought. I had come to America to earn a master's degree, find a job and hopefully earn enough money to send back home. It would be years before I would have the opportunity to act on the thought of immersing myself in the wonderful world of commerce and retail.

2014

I left New York City in 2011 to wade into the technology and start-up scene in India. I had quit my job and career in the US to come back to India to work with my friend Deepinder Goyal (Deepi) who had started a company called Foodiebay a few years earlier. The company, now called Zomato, had just raised its first round of venture capital. I decided to join Zomato as I felt that India was fast becoming the land of opportunity if one wanted to build something for themselves. Every time I returned from America to visit, I noticed that there was a sea change in the way things were previously. Cities were becoming bigger, the internet was proliferating and so were smartphones. What I learnt at Zomato only made it more obvious to me that things were changing at home. My itch to become an entrepreneur was becoming more acute and, in 2014, I decided to venture away from Zomato and start Grofers.

At the time, Flipkart was already a six-year-old business, and Amazon had recently entered the market, adding to the number of e-commerce players, such as Snapdeal, leading the e-commerce wave. While I still held an interest in working in e-commerce, it seemed more sensible to chase the opportunity that had presented itself rather than go after my passion.

Back then, Grofers was a really small business trying to find its feet. We served shops in local markets by providing a common on-demand delivery service. We onboarded local shops (such as grocery stores, chemists and hardware stores) who would use our technology platform to punch in the orders they received over the phone or WhatsApp from their customers. The platform would then send an SMS to a delivery partner, whom we employed, who would pick up the product from the shop and deliver it to the customer. We had thirty delivery partners who worked with Grofers.

Then, one day, only sixteen turned up.

The absenteeism of our employees had led me to visit the hub of Amazon Transportation Services (ATS), a vertical of Amazon

India that handles their deliveries to customers. I was holding a pamphlet that Amazon had put up at various locations around Gurgaon (now Gurugram), in the National Capital Region (NCR), including right outside our tiny office (which we called a station) in the middle of Sushant Lok. The pamphlet was essentially a recruiting call from Amazon for delivery partners at their nearby hub. Its headline promised earnings of ₹25,000 per month for the partners selected to join them. As compared to this promising salary, we were paying only a shade above minimum wage, around ₹12,000 per month at the time (minimum wage at the time was around ₹332 per day or around ₹10,000 per month).[1] The Amazon ad looked too good to be true compared to what the rest of the market was paying for the job. Most folks doing deliveries were paid close to half the minimum wage (₹7,000 per month) in the informal market. We were barely able to break even as a small business while paying minimum wage, so it was incomprehensible how this proposition from Amazon could be profitable for them.

I decided to investigate and made my way to the ATS hub closest to us. There, next to a small fan in a large, empty godown, sat the hub incharge. I told him what I did and that my little new start-up was under threat because we would lose all our partners to Amazon if their business could afford to pay ₹25,000 per month for a delivery job. Of course, as a large company, they could afford to pay more than double the going rate, but my concern was whether it was a temporary phenomenon or if they were structurally secure enough to always pay delivery partners much higher wages than we could afford. If the latter were true, our business would really struggle to compete. The market wages we anticipated for delivery would be reset to a higher level, and we would find it difficult to convince small businesses to pay us more, which, in turn, would make the delivery businesses in local markets largely unviable. We were already competing with an unorganized sector where deliveries were done by informal workers who were paid in cash, and in almost all cases paid way below the minimum wage.

As it turned out, I was looking in the wrong direction. The hub in-charge, a young guy not even thirty years old, was irritated, sweaty and amused, all at the same time. In an ode to countless workers on the frontline in countless organizations around the world, he started complaining to me about invisible management teams taking decisions while they were far removed from the ground realities. The 'management', he said, had introduced this payout structure and essentially the 'management' had no idea how things really worked.

The ad on the pamphlet had said the partners would get paid ₹25,000 if they worked twenty-six days in a month and did not take a single unscheduled leave. However, since the minimum wage rules applied (they were employees of a manpower service provider), they would get paid minimum wage as long as they turned up on at least twenty-one days. The 'powers that be' at Amazon were trying to stop unscheduled absenteeism by almost doubling the pay for delivery partners. But, as it turned out, the lucrative thing about the job was not the ₹25,000 being paid for twenty-six days of work but the ₹12,000 that was a surety for twenty-one days of work. To top it all, the hub in-charge confided that he was being questioned by his supervisors as to why the rate of unscheduled absenteeism was going up instead of decreasing despite the higher payouts that were promised.

As my understanding of micro-economics gently crumbled in the background, I found myself struggling to grasp this mindset and social behaviour. It was perhaps also the first moment when I realized that building a business in India, one that dealt with Indian problems, Indian customers and Indian infrastructure, would require a much deeper understanding of the social, economic and political contexts within which I was trying to build.

Over the years, realizations like this and many others have shaped my comprehension of the Indian landscape—one that is constantly evolving as millions of people rise out of poverty, move to urban areas, overcome centuries of discrimination and try to create better lives for themselves and their families. As a nation, we made a big pivot in the 1990s when liberalization kicked in to prevent a teetering economy from collapsing. The after-effects of that change—increased opportunity and development—were also accompanied by clear side-effects, such as wealth disparity, toxic cities, strained infrastructure, to name just a few. At the same time, the economic forces that shape and explain behaviours in society have a hard time reconciling the socialist mindset of the Indian working class with the new paradigm of meritocracy and capitalism. Just as ten years ago I had stood at the beginning of my American experience, learning new things about society, ideologies, commerce and the way things got done, now I was standing at the beginning of my Indian entrepreneurial journey, learning these things all over again. This time around, I was trying to build a business in a place which did not seem to behave like I had expected it to and where I still felt like an observer on the outside, trying to figure out the things that would help me understand it better. All this still in pursuit of success—success that would enable me to move ahead in life and manifest itself in my ability to build a business here.

2024

It was almost midnight on 24 March 2024, the eve of Holi. A few people from the early days of Grofers, including me, were huddled around a standing table on the roof of Rishi Arora's (my co-founder at Blinkit, and one of the first people to join Grofers back in 2014)· house in Gurgaon. Around us, there was a party in full swing but the six of us stood staring at a single phone, watching the numbers updating on the screen. We were not tracking stocks or bets—we were looking at the number of orders placed on Blinkit before midnight. Every few seconds the screen would refresh and we would get closer to a million orders for the day. It was now a race against the clock—would this be the first time we would exceed a million orders or would we have to wait a few more days to reach that milestone? With minutes to go, the orders crossed the million mark. We cheered, high-fived and went back to the party. It had taken ten years for Blinkit (formerly called Grofers) to go from zero orders to processing a million a day, all delivered within ten minutes of the customer placing the order. It felt like a watershed moment. Less than six months later, we would reach 2 million orders in a day. We had found a place in the halls of commerce on the back of delivering thousands of products to customers in India, within ten minutes as promised. It felt incredible to have built something that seemed as magical to customers as Amazon and Walmart had to me two decades ago.

Amazon now faces off with Blinkit every day and Walmart owns Flipkart, another Indian company with a storied history that is figuring out ways to change this country. I am lucky to have started and built a company that can be discussed in this hallowed group, and in a sector I first discovered as a consumer but one in which I have deep faith. Commerce, I feel, is the measure of integration that we have with the larger society around us (no wonder the proxy wars that are fought these days are mostly called trade wars), and with Blinkit we were now in a position to influence this. To pass on the learnings from this journey is the objective of this book. Giving context to the situations in which these learnings emerged is the task that I am trying to accomplish. My hope is that it will give those of us trying to build in India, in whatever capacity, some ideas about what to expect and how to analyse the business landscape.

The way businesses were built in India started to change in lockstep with the adoption and operation of a new paradigm, which I witnessed for an entire decade while building Blinkit. I grew up in Punjab during the 1980s. At the time, the state was gradually making its way through the aftermath of terrorism and the accompanying restrictions on regular life. Entrepreneurship was viewed as an impossible path for people whose backgrounds were similar to mine, coming as I did from a Sikh farming family in a small village. From those origins, to gain an understanding of the complex way in which India moves forward and how businesses get built here has been a learning experience, complete with lessons in humility and perspective. The way a bunch of people from diverse backgrounds got together to create an organization that has impacted the lives of millions of people is a story filled with deeply gratifying experiences.

I could never relate to business books about entrepreneurship in Western markets or in China. The principles of operating and entrepreneurship mentioned in them did not seem relevant for India a lot of the time. I felt a constant disconnect with these narratives because they talked about building a business in ways that did not work in the Indian context. Yes, many mental models related to how things should be done are applicable universally, but for them to be relevant and effective we need a deeper understanding of the environment we work in.

At the outset, I would like to point out that businesses are not built in a vacuum, away from the social, political and environmental context of the people who are building the businesses or those who are using the end products—the customers. To the extent possible, it is important to be aware not only of the ramifications of these factors on business but also that businesses play a part in changing an existing environment.

This book is an attempt to highlight some of the India-specific anomalies and behaviours that I have come across over the last ten years while building Blinkit and Grofers. The lessons I learnt are nothing new. However, I hope that understanding the circumstances in which these lessons were learnt and hearing my perspective on the factors that shaped these learnings, will help the readers of this book think deeply and differently about them.

As I thought about certain problems, some of the unusual aspects of building a business in India shifted my perspective. When I look back I find that the biggest lessons for me always centred on a few themes:

Trust: Building trust across different vectors in the Indian ecosystem—with employees, customers, gig workers and communities—is incredibly impactful in the absence of institutional trust as our economy develops.

Belief: Not just a founder's belief in ideas or one's own abilities but also inculcating a similar belief in the people who join and build new companies has been one of the biggest changemakers for the Indian start-up ecosystem and something that we still need to encourage using different financial and social tools.

Clarity: Opportunity in India exists because of the current state of development and the resulting dysfunctions. We can't wish away sub-par infrastructure, archaic regulations, insufficient skilled talent or the many other problems that businesses here still face. It is precisely the difficulty of building a business in the face of these problems that creates the opportunity to set up meaningful and impactful businesses. In this environment, having a long-term mindset and an objective view on what matters, what doesn't and what needs to be solved becomes essential.

Resilience: The existing way in which different elements of our society, infrastructure, governance and businesses interact will have to change if a country the size and scale of India is to make the kind of progress that will improve the standard of living of millions of people. What we are witnessing is the first wave of disruption that is going to challenge a number of things—our beliefs, ways of doing business, regulations and social structures. Things that succeeded elsewhere in the world might not work here, and vice versa. In an environment that is this dynamic and constantly evolving, the ability of founders and start-ups to stay the course, adapt and innovate will be the single-biggest driver of impactful outcomes, and one that I hope can be strengthened by discussing it more openly.

Alongside, I wanted to tell the story of building Blinkit (and Grofers) and its people and culture. Over the years, Blinkit has evolved as an organization that is the outcome of discovering more of the world around us. We learnt about inequality and opportunity at the bottom of the pyramid; we learnt how to pick and ignore certain problems; we learnt how to spend our time creating systems that would power us for decades; and we learnt about the needs of our customers as well as the genesis of those needs. We were learning all this while struggling or flourishing as a company and dealing with internal dysfunctions as well as macro-environment changes that we had no control over.

I wanted to document these lessons from the first decade of Blinkit's existence before they faded from memory and inspire more entrepreneurs and builders in a way that is realistic but hopeful. I do believe that more ambitious entrepreneurship, sincerity towards making real progress by creating long-term systems, creating inclusive and meritocratic cultures and increasing the size of the opportunity pie will help India change meaningfully. Our company, Blinkit, is an example of what is possible with the relentless pursuit of these ideals with clear eyes, full hearts and resilience that is powered by an objective view of the world—it isn't just a pipe dream.

The greatest joys over the last twenty years or so of seeing India, first through the lens of a fresh graduate looking for employment and then through a founder's, have been the emerging opportunities for a meritocratic path to success. The people who have built Blinkit are the greatest source of pride and satisfaction for me. Most of them were not born into great privilege but made a small start-up into a disruptive and large organization that has a real impact on the lives of millions of people. Such success stories, which are not dependent on one's background, used to be a trickle back in the day, but their number is steadily increasing and they deserve a place in the headlines. For people like me, the world changed within ten years of starting a company. When I talk to folks who built their organizations before liberalization and the dot-com boom, more often than not they say this is a world they never imagined would exist in India.

These experiences and lessons from my journey are presented so that more builders can find the courage to take on the challenges this country poses. True progress for our country will be the result of economic opportunity created by many and will be enabled by an understanding of how the world of technology and that of everyday operations in India merge. This is essential for dreaming up large outcomes.

If you are a builder reading this book, I hope you will find in these pages some inspiration that helps you make sense of the chaos and the tough days that inevitably come as part of the journey of enterprise. You could be working in a manufacturing company, a technology company, or building a brand-new services business—but I hope you will find something to take away from reading this. This book is not a 'how-to' manual for overcoming the challenges of entrepreneurship in India, but a realistic picture of the 'why' and 'what could work'. What I have put down on these pages worked for me and everyone who has played a part in building Blinkit. While, like so many others, I started out on this path seeking personal success and wealth, over the years there have been enough moments of failure at achieving both that have made me appreciate the necessity and the truths of building in India. I think more people will build if they are encouraged to embrace the realities and pain of building. The first step is to learn about them.

25 DECEMBER 2013

THE BEGINNING

I was sitting at Nini's Snacks And Tea Stall in the Sushant Shopping Arcade in Gurgaon. At the time, I was heading international operations at Zomato, the company founded by my childhood friend Deepi. I had just returned from an exhausting multi-country trip and had dragged my jetlagged self to the market to find out how another one of my old friends, Saurabh Kumar (SK), was doing. SK and I used to work together in America and he had started an interesting new venture called Onenumber right here in Gurgaon. The premise was simple: You opened up the Onenumber website and ordered some of the basic groceries on the website, or just typed in whatever you wanted in a comment box, and it would be delivered to you within 30 minutes.

SK had been working on the concept in fits and starts for a few months by then. It was an interesting concept, but getting customers regularly was proving to be challenging. There was one customer who ordered samosas and jalebis from the same sweetshop every day—but given the lifestyle of the customer,

SK wasn't betting on the customer being of high value in the long term. Then there were the occasional orders whenever there were marketing events in some areas of Gurgaon. Meanwhile, SK was spending from his pocket to finance the operations and had also borrowed money from friends and family to get things off the ground. He had pinged me a month ago to tell me more about what he was doing, get some advice and ask for some help with investment in the company.

At the time, I had spent over two years at Zomato, building the international operations, but was also thinking of starting something of my own. This was, however, not why I was at the tea stall. I was there to understand what Onenumber was doing so I could help out a friend. Incidentally, SK and I were joined at the tea stall by one of SK's friends and classmates from college, Nitin Saluja. Nitin had started a cafe chain called Chaayos at the time and was in the process of opening his third outlet. As we sipped tea in the winter sun and discussed Onenumber and how the business was doing, SK mentioned that he was financing the business by also using the two delivery workers in Onenumber to make deliveries from Chaayos's central kitchen to their outlets throughout the day. Chaayos paid him per delivery. Nitin was happy with this arrangement as he didn't have to manage more employees for deliveries and he could pay per delivery whenever he needed to get it done.

After Nitin left, SK and I continued discussing the Onenumber business. That night, as some of the thoughts of the day swirled in my head, I kept going back to how Nitin had repeatedly said that the Onenumber delivery workers were really useful for him. I realized that the reason he was sticking to Onenumber was because he was a very satisfied customer of a service. This on-demand delivery service for another business was not Onenumber's primary offering, though. I messaged the thought to SK; he'd been thinking about it as well, but wasn't sure what could be done with it. That night, I could barely sleep. I kept thinking about creating some sort of an on-demand delivery service that could power local deliveries, similar to how Fedex powered cross-country deliveries in America. If Chaayos was in such need of this, maybe there were a lot of other businesses in the local market that would need the service as well.

Over the next day, SK and I kept going back and forth on what this service would look like, why it would be a better answer for local businesses and how we could potentially make money in the process. By the second night, I was so excited about the idea that I told SK I would leave Zomato and join him to build on our brainwave if he agreed to shut down Onenumber and work exclusively on this idea. SK was convinced. He would shut down Onenumber and rename the company to something that would be more appropriate to what we were going to do.

Late at night on 26 December 2013, I registered the domain grofers.com for ₹599 and built a simple one-page site for what we were going to do. I was looking for the word 'gofer'—which in American parlance meant errand performer—but everything related to that word was too expensive. Channelling the naivete and confidence that come from youth and enthusiasm, we reasoned that if the business worked then the name wouldn't matter, and if it died the name wouldn't have mattered anyway.

SK and I decided that our first task the morning after creating the website would be to go to the local market and start talking to more local businesses about using our two delivery workers for their own local deliveries. We created a prepaid rate card, similar to how mobile companies charged for prepaid plans, and started visiting the local shops. We had a surprisingly good hit rate and were able to sign up our first customer and collect an advance payment from them the same day. Almost immediately, the orders started streaming in. Now we had to deliver them.

We signed up to a commitment of delivering hundreds of orders every day within the first week for a couple of pharmacy stores and Chaayos with only two full-time workers (one of whom disappeared for some time during the day to tend to his booming property dealing side hustle). As we desperately tried to hire more people, SK and I also made deliveries during the day whenever we could find time. Our first customer, a pharmacist, had realized that we had likely overpromised, but he was helpful and patient while we tried to figure out how to do his deliveries on time. We adjusted the delivery time to ninety minutes from the thirty minutes we had ambitiously promised so we could manage the workload better.

After a long day of being on the road and making deliveries, we would spend the night figuring out how to create a better interface for our few customers to place their request for deliveries, so we could move away from pen and paper. At the same time, we had to figure out a way to also manage the delivery workers; they needed to know where to go and what to do without being on phone calls all the time.

As Grofers started consuming more and more of my attention, I told Deepi that I would have to leave Zomato to do this full time. While it was a tough conversation, ultimately, he saw that I really wanted to do this and was supportive. I started spending all my time on Grofers, and SK and I split our responsibilities. I would spend time in the markets signing up more customers while SK would focus on hiring more partners and managing deliveries, and occasionally signing up new customers when he had the time. As we started expanding, the merchant community, through word of mouth, began sending us contacts for a number of different businesses that needed a service like ours. First, there were the chemists, then the pharmacy distributors, then grocery shops and even small businesses that wanted paperwork delivered locally.

Within a month, we were signing up merchants faster than we were able to hire delivery partners. All the while, our 'office hours' were from 8 a.m. to 11 p.m. and then we would go back home and start working on the systems part of it, including trying to find more people who could help us with the technology and operations bit. The exhilaration of growth and the number of things that needed to be done every day left us little time to think of anything else.

In about five months we were making more than five hundred deliveries daily in just a small area of Gurgaon, serving only three local markets. Most of our business then involved delivering from local shops to customers, with a few businesses also using us to deliver to other businesses. Around this time, the reality of building in India started creeping into our everyday lives. Little did I know then that the company's journey and my personal journey of learning would only accelerate from there.

2014

TRUST AT THE BOTTOM OF THE PYRAMID

I was standing in a 14-foot-by-10-foot shop in the middle of Gurgaon's Sushant Lok area. Somewhere among the tightly packed shops of Sushant Shopping Arcade was the Grofers office in early 2014, when we were a small, barely profitable business trying to build a hyper-local delivery network for our clients—local merchants like grocery stores and chemist shops. The room had a shelf full of helmets, a long bench where our delivery partners could sit and rest between their orders and a table with a single laptop that my co-founder, SK, or I would use to operate our dashboard to manage the orders that were coming in from local stores. The table was also where we answered phone calls from local merchants, who were angry or hassled most of the time. We followed up on the progress of deliveries happening via our network, collected and counted the cash that was flowing in through the network and, after hours, would occasionally also use the table as a bar counter for whatever liquor we could afford.

The atmosphere in the small room in the middle of summer was easy-going and most people preferred the open corridor outside to sitting inside the stuffy little room. The office (which we used to call a station) had about fifteen or twenty delivery partners at any given time. They were mostly in their early twenties, a mix of locals and migrants, primarily from the states of Bihar, West Bengal and Uttar Pradesh. The delivery partners also socialized with each other along those regional lines. The migrants would not sit inside the office if the locals were there, preferring instead to hang out at a tea stall (the unsaid agreement was that the locals had the first right to the shelter of the station). This wasn't to suggest that there was unity within the grouping by state. There were frequent flare-ups along caste lines or regional lines, most often in relation to a disagreement over a subject that would seem innocuous to me.

This was my first time dealing with a large number of unskilled people in entry-level jobs, and we were trying to figure out how a business such as ours, which was so dependent on this workforce, could scale. Not unlike the problem that Amazon was facing in the introduction to this book, we were suffering from unpredictability. We had started the business a few months ago with two delivery partners, with SK and me pitching in to deliver packages for our clients—the local shops. Now we had nearly thirty delivery partners and we served close to a hundred businesses with our logistics service. However, on any given day, we weren't sure how many of our employees would turn up. We spent an inordinate amount of time every day trying to call people and get them to come in for their shift, or hiring new people when those on the payroll abruptly stopped showing up. The phrase used by operations teams and human resources teams for this behaviour was 'employee is absconding'. It was perhaps meant to scare employees into thinking that not showing up for work unannounced was a criminal act, but I don't think it had any impact on the ground.

We promised timely and reliable delivery to the local businesses that we served and having this sort of unpredictability in attendance led to a lot of stress every day. It also took time away from things we could do to grow the business. Due to the unpredictability, we could not estimate if we'd be able to serve all the requests we received on a certain day, or even serve a single one. Some of the local shops relied on us for important deliveries like insulin, so we had to make sure our service was always available. For us and our new business, every day was an anxious experience.

A typical day for us started at 8 a.m. with either SK or me opening the station and then waiting for the first delivery partner to arrive. Some had a reporting time of 9 a.m. and were supposed to report fifteen minutes before the work shift started. Unlike today, where most delivery companies operate on a gig model (pay per order), back in the day, every delivery partner was an employee of the company.

The orders that the merchants placed would start streaming in before 9 a.m. as they had their customers waiting for deliveries. Grocery and pharmacy shops especially had high demand at the beginning of the day itself.

The routine was the same every day. Not a single person would show up till almost 10 a.m. and we would be guessing whether anyone was going to show up at all to do the deliveries. If there was only one of us at the shop, we wouldn't be able to go and do the deliveries ourselves as the rolling shutter of the station would have to be put down. In that case, the delivery partners would not wait around—probably assuming we had shuttered the business and left.

Besides, to grow the business, we also had to go out every day for sales (to sign up more clients), so we needed the delivery partners to show up on time and on schedule.

Faced with the issue of absenteeism and delivery partners not reporting on time, we had already tried multiple incentives and disincentives. We tried to deduct salaries (which led to strikes and fights), we tried to pay bonuses for coming in on time (which worked on a small fraction of our delivery partners), we tried to move shift timings, and so on. Everything we tried to execute from our understanding of the way professionalism was supposed to work did not work. Our college-educated privilege was a long way off from the everyday lives of the people we were employing.

I wanted to learn about their lives and how to work with this workforce. Little did I know that my quest to understand the ecosystem of the large unskilled workers in India would be multifaceted, complex and sometimes heartbreaking. At the same time, I did not know that I was going to witness a paradigm change in this segment that was going to be a factor in building the company.

The first large issue was that for the vast majority of delivery partners, life was full of unpredictability. And this unpredictability flowed into our operations. It originated due to two factors—their social and their economic circumstances. If a child fell sick or someone in the family needed to visit a hospital, it usually meant a demand on their time that could not be passed along to someone else. A lot of the 'outside home' work was done exclusively by men and therefore, when such a need arose, the working person had to opt for absenteeism (this is markedly more prevalent in India's northern and western states than the southern or eastern ones). Very often, tasks relating to childcare, healthcare or any kind of interface with institutions were time consuming and involved waiting in line with no formal systems to ease the process. The support services available to them were inefficient at best (like healthcare) or totally deficient (like childcare). In turn, these unexpected events affected our operations. More importantly, it severely impacted the delivery partners' own ability to hold down formal jobs.

The economic circumstances were a lot clearer. The low level of wages in general in the informal sector and the overall lower wage levels across the country meant that a lot of people did not have an economic cushion if unexpected expenses arose. A flat tyre could put a person out of employment for weeks if they couldn't afford to get a new one for their motorcycle. Something as simple as not having money to get their bike repaired would mean they would move to a different job till they could make the money, get their motorcycle repaired and start doing deliveries again.[1] Savings were rarely built up as most of the earnings were sent back home or spent on essential things like home maintenance or festivals, or seemingly non-essential things like alcohol or fashion. Usually they managed to subsist on the minimum wage but that rarely left them with any money to try to raise their standard of living, or to invest in something that could help them supplement their wages. Economic opportunities were also usually local and limited—with not much scope of earning more than they already did.

Sometimes, the stories we heard were downright real and painful and, occasionally, they were blatant lies to cover up a lack of seriousness about the job. Whatever the reason, the predictability of our business was hurt every time the unpredictability of the lives of our delivery workers came into the picture.

Over time, we could make out the segmentation among our delivery partners well. Migrants and people with kids in their families were the most reliable, that is, more likely to adhere to their shift times and not take leaves without any notice. They were on a mission to make money to send back home, or needed predictable cash flow to keep their household functioning. They were usually slightly older and had real responsibilities. Since most of the folks working as delivery partners were not very well educated, they realized that hard physical labour was their best shot at making ends meet. In that sense, they considered a job with us, where they earned enough and had to make their rounds on a motorcycle, a step up in life. Their manual tasks were limited to riding around on a bike and delivering orders. They were also realistic enough to realize that earning ₹13,000 to ₹15,000 per month doing deliveries was one of their best options as most other jobs requiring manual labour paid less than half of that. They were committed to the work but were also the first ones to jump ship the moment someone else paid them slightly higher wages, even if the level of effort was higher. Over the years, this is the segment that has powered most of India's home delivery revolution.

The bachelors from the local communities seemed to be the ones who had the most demands on their time—whether to back up a friend in a fight, or to help a relative, or just have a night out with the boys. They were also the ones most unserious about the job, since they almost universally treated a delivery job as a stopgap till something better arrived. They had not left their homes in search of an opportunity; they were waiting for a better opportunity in their homes. They usually treated the delivery work as extra cash, and had their lives more or less taken care of at home. It felt as though the demographic dividend of the country was being wasted, just waiting for a better thing to turn up.

This better opportunity, for bachelors, locals or migrants, was universally a government job. We had aspirants for clerks in different departments of the local or state governments, candidates for police jobs, holders of engineering degrees preparing for an entrance exam for a state job. I am not surprised anytime there is a story in the news about thousands of people appearing for a handful of entry-level government jobs.[2] In the small sample set of delivery partners I had worked with, it was clear that entry-level government jobs, or even outsourced contractual government work, ranked much higher in prestige, stability and aspiration than a better-paying job in private enterprise. More on this later.

As mentioned earlier, the migrants were motivated by a stable source of money but were willing to change jobs if another one that paid slightly more came along. They didn't even seem to mind if that job required more manual labour. When it came to predictability, we soon realized that if a migrant employee did not show up one day, chances were he would never show up again. He would have moved on to a better opportunity.

The locals were also doing it for the money, but they were not attached to the job or motivated by it—they were just waiting for the next big thing to come along. When I sat down with them to discuss their lives, they were rarely forthcoming on details of their personal circumstances. Apart from learning that they had a child or two, it was very hard to get any more information about their personal lives. I think a part of it was distrust of someone from the outside, like me, and the other part was probably some element of pride, that they would be seen as 'poor' in their own city. What was not hard to get out of them were the different ways you could go about getting a government job, or the process of getting something like a caste certificate made, or even how the different state- and national-level pension schemes worked. There was always a distrust of government, but the government was also seen as a source of income that set you up for life—if someone were to benefit from that government job, it might as well be me, was their thought process.[3] Ambitious people were not coming to work with us because working harder here made little sense to them—they didn't think it would lead to the same security or progress as a government job.

For a lot of young people (and mostly men) in India, it is a socially perceived notion that the government is the biggest employer. However, in reality, government jobs are vastly outnumbered not only by the applicants, but also by the openings available in other sectors. Mindsets and folk knowledge, however, take time to catch up with data and the reality. We opened up our economy in the 1990s but it seems like we forgot to tell our people what a more capitalistic society looks like. A large section of the people we interacted with every day weren't cheering for the private sector or for acceleration in the development of the economy. Even though they were aware that government jobs were dwindling, a number of them still held out hope that they would get one.

The most common characteristic among both the locals and migrants, however, was the poor level of education and skill. Only rarely would we encounter someone who we thought was overqualified for a delivery job. The reading and writing skills of many partners who worked with us in the early days, even those with college degrees on paper, were barely adequate to get the job done. We used to put up a lot of announcements on the general board in the station in the early days. It was fairly common for delivery partners to wait for someone among them who knew how to read well to come along, to make sure they got the message right. While in 2014, almost everyone was getting adept at using entry-level smartphones, the usage and functionality were restricted to music apps, Facebook, or a basic understanding of the Grofers delivery-partner app. We realized very early on that basic education had failed to reach most of the people who were working with us, and that whatever education had reached them was not the equivalent of skill.

The second common characteristic was that both the locals and migrants viewed life at home as the most comfortable option and the dream state. For migrants, the conversations were always around saving enough to permanently move back to the idyllic existence of their villages and subsequently work in agriculture for subsistence. For locals, since opportunity, in the form of urban development, had expanded to reach their villages, they had chosen to stay at home. While I could relate to the yearning for the familiarity of home, the economic reason they gave was harder to understand. Their reasoning was that the money that they earned in the city got them more in their hometown or village. For instance, savings of ₹1,00,000 meant being able to subsist for more than a year in the villages whereas it would likely not even last half that time in the cities.[4] The drive was not to earn more for progress but to earn enough to work less. This was the back-up plan if a government or 'pukka' job didn't turn up. Access to better healthcare, better schools or better economic opportunity in the cities was not in their consideration when they thought about quality of life.

A career option that was a distant second for some was a job at the Maruti or Hero automobile manufacturing factories in Gurgaon. I think, globally, people want the security of a big-name company or the government when they think about stable jobs. Even if the trade-off is a lower salary or a more procedural job with a lower ceiling, they don't want the anxiety that their employer might go bust some day or, worse, ask them to leave. I am not generalizing the work here—in economies with weak trust in the systems, sometimes being part of larger systems is the only way for people to overcome this everyday anxiety.

So, we were dealing with a workforce that was looking for stable jobs, preferably with the government, were not educated or skilled enough, had no institutional support systems and led very unpredictable day-to-day lives which made it hard for them to fit into formal employment. Inspired by our insights into this workforce, I wanted to find out who had actually dealt with and overcome these issues of working with this workforce. That research inevitably led to factories that operated around Gurgaon at the time, whose management appeared to be getting it right. I went on a fact-finding mission as to why a large number of workers at factories like those of Hero or Maruti managed to show up on time, whereas we had issues with a handful of delivery partners. These factories were also private enterprises that operated with a large segment of unskilled or semi-skilled workers—and seemed to rank higher for job aspirants than we did, albeit still lower than a government job—the 'pukka' jobs.

I met a few people who worked in these large factories to try to understand how we could do a better job at making our operations more predictable. We wanted to put in place systems that would motivate our people to be regular and communicative, and take the job seriously as a building block of life.

The first person I met was responsible for an auto-component manufacturer's factory workers, and gave me useful insights. According to him, the factory workers felt that there was a sense of permanence in their jobs. A large complex with infrastructure and a sense of community reinforced that feeling. They saw a future for themselves in that factory, even if that future entailed that they did the same job for the next twenty years as the presence of the factory alone was a physical marker of predictability—a benefactor-government-light model. There would be a steady income stream based on which they could build their lives and some incentive measures like health insurance for families would be an added benefit although it was rarely valued or available. Most formal employers in the industrial space also eventually reverted to providing government social security programme-led benefits. This made predictability the biggest asset of a factory job.

Predictability, then, encourages employees to make an effort to adhere to timings while lowering absenteeism. Even so, most factories made it a point to not hire locals because of the burden of management that came along with hiring them (in any part of the country). Most of the factories that I came across would hire migrants from far flung areas and provide them with accommodation and food to make sure adherence to work timings was maintained. It is almost comical that setting up factories also comes with this cross-border migration from one state to the other. Factories in Orissa (now Odisha) will hire from Bihar but factories in Haryana will hire from Orissa. This was the solution that factories had figured out over the years for the problem of managing social status dynamics in different areas. If you didn't know anyone in the area, then the likelihood of you worrying about the social status or nature of the job was less. As a number of factories also invested in food and accommodation for the migrants, they also had a higher level of control over the habits of their employees. In short, these factories were trying to reduce unpredictability in their own operations by reducing unpredictability in the lives of the people that they hired. A steady income stream was a source of predictability, set shift timings were a source of predictability and so were the other benefits these employers provided. The section of people whose lives were supremely unpredictable were being shown a Garden of Eden where the currency wasn't actually more money (which capitalism promised); rather, it was the promise of predictability in income and routine.

For the employees, being far away from home also made their lives more predictable. They stayed in hostels, were shuttled to the factories in buses and, at the end of the shift at a specified time, returned to the same place where they also formed bonds of community. Everyone was gravitating towards a system which gave predictability to both sides. Seeing a massive factory in front of you was an image of permanence that was hard to get rid of. There was also the added element of pride in being a worker at a large factory versus working for a small local shop or small organization.

The factory manager also told me that the typical buffer they had in manpower was fairly high (north of 10 per cent).[5] Even with unplanned exigencies, with such a large number of workers, the operations of the factory remained relatively unaffected. This brought out an interesting dynamic in how these buffers inhibited the working class in India from upskilling.

The reason these factories existed in the first place as manufacturing hubs was due to the availability of a high number of unskilled workers willing to work at lower wages than global benchmarks. The cost of additional buffers in headcount was baked into the economics of the products that these factories made. Over the years, they had set up elaborate hiring practices from different parts of the country, coupled with providing hostels and food, and pricing in redundancies—all factors that led to relatively lower unpredictability in available manpower. When you studied this over a long enough period though, the manpower was still unpredictable. People would go home and not come back for the job or disappear one day because they got an opportunity closer to home. In some cases, they had 'moved up' to government jobs. This meant there were no upskilling programmes for these workers at the factories. Companies did not want to invest in upskilling an unreliable workforce, so most of the factory workers stayed range-bound in economic opportunity and only a few had any sort of a career progression.

There were some who benefitted from developing on-the-job skills and moved up, but the numbers appeared to be extremely low. The constant influx of people moving from informal to formal employment also meant that demand and supply were never an issue.

The second person I met during my fact-finding mission around factory work operated a large garment-manufacturing factory, which primarily exported products to global markets. They introduced me to their enforcer. If the worker didn't show up or did not show up on time, the enforcement team would show up at their doorstep to ask them why. The message was clear to the workers: If you want to get paid, show up for work. While I couldn't quite make out whether violence was used, I am fairly certain that that was the subtext of the message being delivered to the workers. Either way, it seemed like a very inefficient system with rows and rows of line managers just looking at people working and not really contributing.

Put off by the second approach, I realized we needed to become a place where people saw a future even if they were working as delivery partners. I was desperate to introduce some sort of predictability into our system even though we could never build an edifice of predictability like a factory (all our workers were scattered around the city most of the day—the company was basically an app they interacted with). I reckoned that the job of the delivery partner had to take on elements that gave it some respectability as a career, if we were to scale up our company. Sure, we would probably only be appealing to the migrants but having a more stable relationship with migrants would be a better situation than the one we were in at the time. My learning from the whole exercise was that we needed to create more than just the opportunity of work for people. We also had to figure out how to make the opportunity predictable enough, valuable enough and respectable enough to get wilful participation.

We chalked up a plan that would add these elements to the job of a delivery partner. In addition to the mandatory Provident Fund (PF) and Employees' State Insurance Corporation (ESIC) contributions, we would contribute some amount every month towards a fund that delivery partners who worked for more than a year with us would be able to tap into for their children's school fees. We also made a promise that as we got bigger and added more clients, we would open up more career progression roles for the delivery partners, including managing the stations and having the opportunity to earn more by learning new skills—like operating a computer and making spreadsheets.

We thought that providing opportunities for upskilling would inspire some people to also invest in themselves while they earned a living with us. At least, they would be motivated to not be absent even when someone was willing to pay a higher salary for just a day. We wanted to give them visibility on the long-term and provide something other opportunities did not.

I gathered all the delivery partners one morning to lay out our plans and hopefully get a handful of them to believe in the merits of long-term employment with our fledgling company. We were signing up more and more local businesses who wanted to use our service and I was hoping that all the delivery personnel would have seen the growth happening around them and would feel that this was the place to be. The purpose of my speech was to make them realize that they had a growth opportunity in front of them and that we were also committing to their long-term benefit. Here we were, a small company, investing whatever little resources we had in creating a better outcome for our employees—we did feel noble, I won't lie.

In the small and stuffy room, I tried to conjure up my best version of a motivating speech to the thirty-odd people. While I was showing them the vision of a better tomorrow, SK was silently sitting in the back, trying to stop himself from rolling his eyes. He did not believe that anyone in the room would take us seriously.

I spoke passionately to a largely stoic room. I didn't have a speech prepared but had thought I would build off the questions that would inevitably stream in when I announced our ground-breaking initiatives. Unfortunately, only a couple of folks asked questions about our plans to set up the 'educating the children' initiative but, overall, there was no significant reaction—good or bad. I was not expecting a standing ovation, but I was hoping that there would be cheerful and curious faces. Instead, everyone got back to doing what they had been doing and the meeting (and my supposedly well-thought-through speech) was quickly forgotten.

Within a month or so of this incident, almost the entire fleet of delivery partners to whom I had made this impassioned plea had quit the company. They had left for other delivery jobs or simply disappeared without any intimation. During that month, we saw zero improvement in absenteeism or unannounced resignations. It made me question my learnings and wonder if we would ever be able to get reliable labour participation in a job that was not housed in the premises of a facility. What was it about their behaviour that we did not understand? Clearly, intimidating workers to come to work was not my cup of tea, so I looked for better answers.

Unfortunately, there were no large mysteries about the delivery personnel behaviour that I was able to figure out by talking to a few of the people who had left. The common refrain was simply that they didn't trust us. We couldn't control the unpredictability of their life, but we couldn't even build a connection with them that would make them trust us on our word.

This was our larger problem that had not been solved anywhere in the ecosystem. Any long-term promises that we were making were only as good as our standing as a brand in society. If a large brand was going to get up and make a claim for a brighter future, the workers would have given it some credibility. Two guys in a 200-square-foot room with a broken air conditioner making those claims accounted for nothing. They were simply letting us know with their silence that they didn't believe us or care about believing us. They left not because we were failing, but because they didn't believe we could succeed.

The promises of the private sector were only as good as the respect of the brand, and were still topped by a government job. A large brand like TATA has built that equity over the years where the workforce will believe in whatever the company says and will hold onto their promise. But when it comes to brands that are new-age or one that is not in the commonly known domain, the willingness of the entry-level workforce to trust them is fairly low. It is only recently that opportunities at emerging companies have started multiplying, especially for those at entry-level wages, so this is a new learning for most of the ecosystem. However, the lack of trust at the entry level remains a problem for newer businesses trying to scale up.

This lack of trust is not without reason.

There was enough history of the exploitation of the poor and marginalized in the country, especially due to the prevalence of the caste system and class-based discrimination, and the resulting inequity has heightened this lack of trust.[6] That is why you don't see the labour laws play any part in the local informal economy, which is still the largest employer in the country.

There are also plenty of unscrupulous hustlers in a country like India, where enforcing the law of the land is still difficult. The folks who are entering the formal workforce at the bottom are often taken for a ride or not paid their basic dues, and when that happens they find that there is no one they can turn to. Hence, the workers don't invest themselves in making the most of the opportunities at emerging companies. This is a vicious cycle—on the one hand it means that emerging employers are constantly frustrated with the quality of the workforce and their discipline. The workers, on the other hand, never believe there is any value to loyalty and discipline as they are perpetually in a situation where organizations are not offering them a path to mastery (and the rewards that come with it) anywhere. The organizations are always dealing in redundancies and therefore don't feel the need to offer that path.

In general, regulations or the labour laws are not able to offer better answers despite their intent. Most of the laws regarding labour in India have been reactive updates to the up-and-coming industry of the time. The laws around industrial labour were updated as new sectors like mining, shipping and exports took hold. However, the laws only kept up with the updated social and political needs, not factoring in the growth of the country's economy or defining central themes. The only exceptions started showing up with the changes that occurred in reaction to the boom in the outsourcing industry. However, those changes were quickly made redundant and started to look archaic as the internet economy, consumer retail, consumption manufacturing and gig work took over. There is simply no way a hundred-year-old structure of the law with multiple confusing edits can keep up with the changing demands of a country's workforce that is now connected to the global economy, the internet and the knowledge it brings. The regulations also fail to take hold when the entire environment, including the social support systems that come with it, does not focus on productivity. Even updating the labour laws will not guarantee that this gap is bridged meaningfully, because the employment-related infrastructure cannot support it effectively. For instance, there is a compulsory requirement in formal employment to provide government-backed health insurance. The fact that it is based on an overstretched healthcare system means that the process to access healthcare takes a lot of time and this leads to a massive loss of productivity to begin with (I am not even taking into account the quality of care). In short, at this point, the regulations and laws are looked at more as a cost of doing business rather than being useful in shaping behaviour in investments or in workers.

In the local market, there is nearly zero investment happening in upskilling the workforce for better productivity. In 2014, according to a National Sample Survey Office report, only 2.2 per cent of the working population in India received any formal vocational training.[7] Small enterprises are unsure of the positive impact of making these investments and the workers are never the beneficiaries, so the system hardly moves forward. This distrust between workers and the rest of society impacts small companies the most. A lack of seriousness from the workers about jobs in small organizations and a subsequent lack of formalization of this working relationship means that jobs at this level are impacted by a lack of professionalism. It means that even small companies operate with redundancies and with a mindset to not look for an upside in productivity improvements or upskilling. Even though they might be complying with minimum wage and formal employment regulations, the way the work is judged and operated is still seen as informal employment. In the majority of cases, they will also not comply with the minimum wage requirements or provide any kind of health insurance or life insurance benefits formally. To illustrate the depth of this issue, only 3.7 per cent of young regular workers have a written contract, with only about 10.2 per cent receiving any kind of social security benefits.[8]

The unpredictability of workforce supply means employers are always better off paying at or near minimum wage, just like in the factories. To put it simply, an employer who doesn't feel confident that you are a dependable employee will hire extra people at all times. This, in turn, means that the employer will look to pay the least amount of money to you because they don't see you as a dependable employee. The employer is also not investing any extra money in your comfort or upskilling because it would add to their cost without any business gain. That investment, if any, will be worth zero when you don't show up or leave for another job.

When early-stage businesses are estimating the cost of operations, the entry-level workforce requirements end up being lower in their estimate as the cost of their unpredictability is not clearly visible or understood. It leads to a lot of heartburn, and in manpower-dependent businesses can even lead to early-stage failures as the actual cost is much higher than the estimated cost. In the early days of our business, if we estimated that we needed ten partners to serve three hundred orders a day, we would have had to hire at least twenty to account for the unpredictability. This meant that the cost of delivery was double of what we would have estimated based on scientific estimates of the time and effort put in to deliver those orders.

This problem isn't unique to a delivery business. A friend of mine operates a restaurant with six serving staff when she knows she only needs four even during her peak hours. Her small business is living with this inefficiency because she has no idea how many people will show up the next day. This hurts her profitability and subsequent ability to re-invest in the business or open more outlets.

Unreliable workforce, deep distrust of small businesses, limited economic opportunity for an unskilled workforce, insufficient investment in upskilling, social exclusion of manual jobs, and archaic regulations—this was the lay of the land in 2014, when the gig economy took off in India. Development, of course, could not wait for society to resolve its trust issues accumulated over millennia of discrimination, colonization, inequality and exploitation.

The gig economy—a multi-dimensional marketplace where demand and supply could match—has proliferated globally over the last fifteen years. The rise of smartphones probably had a significant part to play here as organizations could start relaying instructions over mobile networks which allowed disaggregated workers to perform tasks.[9] What started as a mode of just relaying tasks, soon became a mode to also relay instructions. So, whereas in the early version of gig work, platforms were just passing along requests or orders from customers to the workers on the ground (think a taxi driver getting a request for pick up via a dispatcher, or a plumber on the road getting assigned a new task), soon the platforms also started making the job of the worker easier (by giving directions to the same driver and settling the bill). Of course, the platforms charged a commission for getting the orders and providing the services to the workers. The gig economy was born.

Gig work soon opened up a lot of avenues where companies could offer services on their platform that were fulfilled by anyone who was registered on the platform. Some platforms also offered to match requests for a task to its fulfilment. People who registered on the platform would get paid when they fulfilled the service but were not obligated to report at a certain time or to work at all at any given time. They could choose to accept or reject the gig. This created a free market for the tasks and for the workers who could complete those tasks. Suddenly, shift timings and, by extension, unpredictability were not an enforcement problem. Demand and supply matching became an economic problem that technology was ripe to solve. Economic incentive replaced trust as the defining mechanism between the supply of workers and the demand for workers.

This concept of a marketplace for work and workers really changed a number of paradigms around what employment meant in different countries. For a lot of low-skill jobs in Western countries, it introduced a large supply of people willing to do that work. So, taxi unions in a number of cities were now competing with people who had a car and the time and were willing to offer rides at a cheaper rate than the mandated prices, which were often set via a process opaque to customers.

While gig work was introducing a marketplace for tasks to find workers, at the same time, workers could now choose tasks which were the best use of their time or skills. As mobile phone penetration increased, an increasing number of workers started working on delivery platforms on a gig model, and Grofers also started gravitating towards this answer. This was mostly because there was no alternative solution that ensured workers would be dependable and professional. The companies (including ours) that adopted gig work as a mode of engaging with workers did not bridge the societal trust gap. Instead, we reduced the reliance on trust, making the relationship extremely transactional. You show up and do the job, you get paid immediately. You can choose to work when you want and make your choices on how much you want to work, but there is no long-term career path we are able to offer. In order to attract these workers, we had to compete with every other company that was also offering to pay for their time and effort on the same model. In a little over a year, the amount of money we were paying per delivery to a delivery partner was up almost 50 per cent because we were now competing to pay per delivery against every other platform out there. The upshot though was that absenteeism was no longer a problem. Workers showed up when they knew there would be demand for their services and an earning opportunity, and instead of a pool of limited employees, there were hundreds of them who would be registered. Migrants dominated this economy too, using it as a way to increase economic opportunity for themselves.

In India, gig work took over in areas like delivery jobs because it solved for trust. Mathematically, you can hire someone full-time in India at a salary higher than minimum wage by 20 per cent and the cost of delivery will still be cheaper than the current cost of delivery in gig work.[10] Here, gig work isn't solving for economics, as is commonly believed—it is solving for trust and predictability, for a price. In the gig economy ecosystem, the rules of engagement are a lot clearer, so that either side has free will to engage and the system can run on almost zero trust. Of course, this gets challenged occasionally when companies fail or glitches occur that break the trust, but largely, that has been the impact of the gig economy—providing a common space for companies and workers where trust is not a factor.

This is a feature of the labour market in India, which is also unusual. Gig work—where you get paid by the task (per order/ per ride) instead of getting a fixed salary for the month—is way more lucrative than doing the same job at close to minimum wage in India than almost anywhere in the world. Outside India, gig work primarily came up as a way to supplement one's income or do part-time work and get close to minimum wage when there weren't enough job opportunities that could pay them a full-time minimum wage. According to a BCG survey, only 1–4 per cent of workers on labour-sharing platforms in mature markets (such as America, UK, Germany, Sweden) treat gig work as the primary source of income, while 5–12 per cent of workers in developing markets (such as China, India and Brazil) earn their primary income through digital platforms.[11]

One of the reasons that gig work took off so massively in India was the fact that it provided an opportunity for a lot of unskilled workers to earn significantly more than minimum wage. This option doesn't exist in the organized or unorganized sectors with formal jobs for them.

Most labour-intensive industries had realized they would have to deal with a lack of work ethic and indiscipline, so they built for redundancies and looked for cost leverage in other places (primarily working conditions and lack of wage growth). As gig work became a prevalent form of getting work done, a lot of companies that could shift their way of working to invest in gig work did so, rather than continuing to invest in a space that was inefficient for the current context and was too slow to change. This can be seen in the rise of adoption of gig work by different industries. Since technology-led companies could make this transition the quickest, you see a lot more of them operating in this space. However, in the near future, a similar 'task-based' model of operating will likely pervade a lot more manpower-intensive businesses, especially ones that are disaggregated.

Sector-wise adoption of gig workforce in India

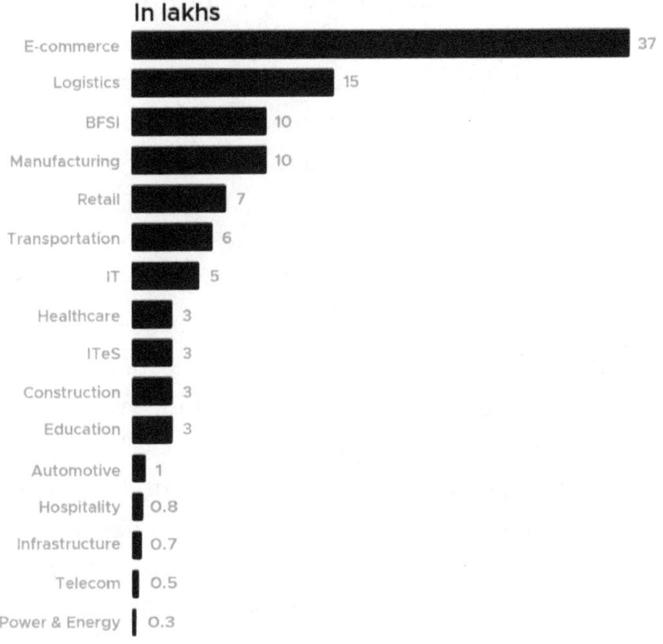

Source: Indian Flexi Staffing Industry Report 2025- Sectoral and State Analysis- Indian Staffing Federation (https://indianstaffingfederation.org/) (As of end of March 2025)

We could argue that Life Insurance Corporation of India (LIC) also operates on a gig model, since their agents work on a task-based model, that is, they earn when they sell a policy. The lines between their way of operating and that of a delivery partner for e-commerce companies will blur as soon as replicable technology platforms make it easier for such companies to incorporate gig work into their operations. We are already seeing this happen in areas such as outsourcing and training of AI models as well. My hope is that the issue of wilful upskilling will get solved by these economic forces and allow workers to earn more in more complicated jobs. But I haven't seen that happen yet.

Almost every company that has been successful with gig work in India has been able to do it when gig work made their operations more predictable for them (or their customers). This allowed the companies to scale, which wasn't possible earlier using a model of employment that just didn't work.

Over the last few years, gig work has become one of the biggest examples of the way market forces have solved the issue of trust at the bottom of the pyramid. When founders and entrepreneurs look at the areas where a developing country like ours has opportunity, it is friction points like these that provide opportunities to solve old problems in new ways. Even today, when we talk about the fact that we are able to run an operationally intensive business with half a million people doing the daily tasks, how we do it efficiently, or without massive management overheads is unfathomable to a number of old-economy companies. It is in part attributable to our ability and willingness to operate with gig workers.

The value of this trade-off for employers in India is high enough that they end up paying way above the wage rate for unskilled workers. The work ethic for employees, though, is enforced via the most capitalistic route (you work, you get paid). For gig workers, there is choice of opportunity and the ability to choose the most lucrative path. For the unskilled worker, it is the place where their manual labour gets paid fair market value based on competition among the different services which need that labour. In a market where formal employment has only seen limited penetration, this is a freedom that has not been easily accessible. The transformation doesn't come without its challenges, though.

Over the years, as Grofers gradually moved some parts of the last-mile ecosystem to a gig-based set-up and started to pay per delivery, we had to adopt a different mindset: The gig worker economy meant that gig workers would have zero trust in us, so transparency and communication were key. We had to invest millions of dollars into our delivery-partner technlogy platforms to make sure our gig workers could see their earnings in real time and the payment systems didn't cause any spikes in anxiety. At the same time, these systems had to operate like a free market price-setting mechanism like the stock market—changing what we were paying according to the mismatch between demand and supply so people would have visibility on earning opportunities.

We also had to make sure that the gig workers always felt that the way they got opportunities to earn was fair and transparent—this also meant that the typical way of looking at performance went out of the window. We had to define a base expectation based on which the partner would be paid for the gig. We could only judge whether the work got done as 0 or 1 against this base expectation. We had no right to expect anything above and beyond this base expectation. Over time, almost all gig systems gravitated towards figuring out how to shape behaviour with incentives and disincentives. At the same time, because the rules of engagement are so objective and deterministic, there is a lot of scope to manipulate these systems as well. This has also led to an endless cycle of figuring out how to close loopholes that allow folks to get away with bad behaviour and make the rules of engagement clearer. For instance, in our systems, we invest significantly in operations, technology and packaging to ensure that products in our supply chain do not go missing—it is an extreme case of preventing bad actors from working in the system which can degrade the end customer's experience. Our learning from doing all this was that gig work as part of the operating principle of the company is a solution for the underlying social issue of attitude towards work and employers, but it isn't any easier to deal with than permanent employment. For the gig workers too, the faceless interface with an app can feel impersonal and tyrannical, making it even more necessary that the platform stay transparent and predictable at all times.

These new ways are not evolutions of existing ways of working, nor are they any kind of answers to the problems of inequity and lack of trust—these are just new answers that operate in a different paradigm. Gig work is a reality of life that is going to be the new way of working in the kind of economies in which we are operating, where the social fabric is still adjusting to rapid economic progress. The fact that there are millions of workers operating as gig workers shows that it is catering to a need in the market for both organizations and workers.

Rise in gig workforce in India

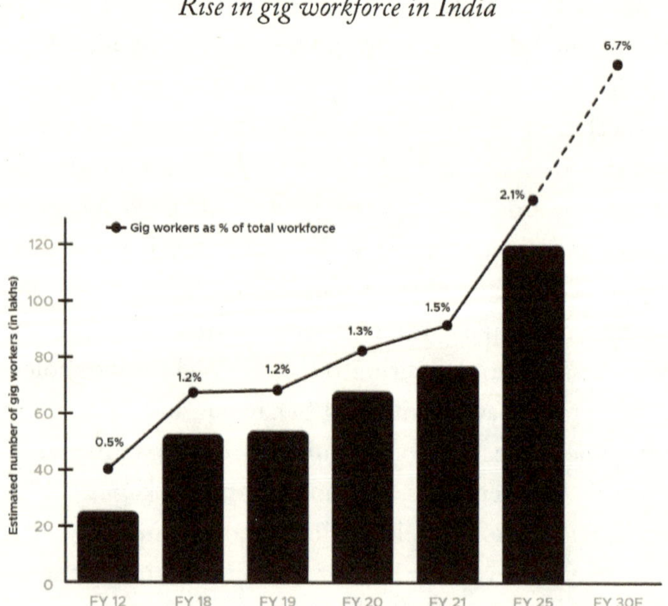

Source: NITI Aayog. (2022). 'India's Booming Gig and Platform Economy: Perspectives and Recommendations on the Future of Work'; Economic Survey 2025-2026. 'Employment and Skill Development: Getting Skilling Right'; UN Department of Economic and Social Affairs. World Population Prospects - India

For some, gig work is a means to earn more, for others it is flexibility in an unpredictable life. For instance, gig workers are heavily over-indexed on the amount of income (46 per cent) and flexible timings (22 per cent) as the top three job drivers compared to non-gig workers (38 per cent and 1 per cent, respectively). Currently, there is no other opportunity that allows an unskilled worker to possibly earn ₹5000 for a day of hard work. It exists in the gig economy.[12]

The expectation of a lot of people from the gig economy is that it is going to look and sound like full-time employment—where individuals gain skills over time, create value and are more appreciated by the organizations. That is an unrealistic expectation from a system which got adopted because it solved other problems for organizations and workers.

A rather different statistic about gig work in India that I have been exposed to—primarily delivery of products or food as a gig—is that it is now increasingly being used as a tool for upward economic mobility. An overwhelming percentage of people who currently work as gig workers here do it in order to supplement their income and not as a way to seek upward mobility in pursuit of something else.[13] This is borne out by the fact that across the organizations that use delivery gig workers, the average time a worker spends working every day is less than four hours. Even when you talk to the gig workers today, the majority of them are doing this job to keep up with something—whether it is an AC repair person looking for incremental income in the slow months or a factory worker trying to make extra money before going to the village for a break, they are all looking to supplement whatever their primary source of earning is, to meet an extra need.

Today, with over half a million delivery partners operating for Blinkit as gig workers, we see the patterns clearly. On average, someone working the equivalent hours of a full-time job on a gig earns around 50 per cent higher than the minimum wage.

However, only about 40 per cent of the overall workforce puts in those full-time hours continuously on gigs. An overwhelmingly large number only work a few hours a day—primarily to augment their income or tide over temporary disruptions in life. Over the years, we have seen more and more partners lean towards using this as their primary source of earning. This is because the partners got used to this way of earning and the companies also learnt more about gig work and started adding features like better health insurance, more flexibility, different ways to generate earning and better infrastructure, which makes the jobs easier. We often hear that workers make sure they work with us for a certain number of hours each month to maintain the private health insurance we provide—something they don't get at their salaried jobs.

Since most of the jobs at the entry level are not going to keep up with inflation and there is hardly any systematic effort behind upskilling, gig work has become the means to add those extra rupees to the bank account every week. Upskilling has been replaced by longer hours outside of primary jobs. I am always surprised when I visit our dark stores and find that some of the delivery partners there are not students or new workers in the city; rather they are people with factory jobs, drivers, retail workers, security guards, restaurant workers. I have even met someone who was a magician by profession.

This has proven that gig work is not just a way to get entry-level workers to earn slightly more and graduate to something else. It is a new kind of employment, which is serving a purpose no other kind of existing employment paradigm is able to solve for people. There is a class of professional gig workers coming up who are using gig work as their primary mode of earning—likely due to the fact that it provides them flexibility in hours or location.[14] Either this is the best use of their skill set or it is a way to balance some other responsibilities in life, which might not be commercial. For instance, the willingness of people in Tier-3 and Tier-4 cities to work on gigs is incredibly high, because it is a way for them to avoid migrating to the larger cities. The nature of the work allows them to care for their families while working on a flexible schedule—an opportunity that did not exist ten years ago. Then there is a class of gig workers who are professionals in a different field and supplementing their earnings with gig work on the side.

The presence of gig work has also led to the transformation of multiple industries. The underlying mobile internet usage has allowed the coordination of a large, disaggregated workforce. This, in turn, has introduced a leap forward in service levels for some industries. You can now get a taxi in almost every town in the country within a few minutes. Less than fifteen years ago, it was almost impossible to find a taxi even in Delhi-NCR. Retailers like Walmart built efficient centralized supply chains riding on the first generation of computing and Amazon centralized it further on the back of internet-generated demand. Quick commerce rode the mobilization of a large workforce via mobile internet to create a decentralized supply chain for goods, which changed the eye level on service completely. Five years ago, thinking of getting almost 40,000 items delivered to you anytime within ten minutes was impossible. It is now an expectation. Innovation and progress follow needs and the path is created by the ecosystems. Just like research and development need robust education and nurturing environments for scientists and tinkerers, a fragmented society has offered entrepreneurs an environment where they can work across these lines and create new business models. The individual might do it for different reasons, but the overall force is pushing towards a permanent change in the way things get done. Gig work is not a distraction but a tool for developing new business models while side-stepping a lot of the prevalent issues (while also bringing up new ones).

This also compares favourably to the progress in attitude towards traditional jobs. The unskilled worker doesn't start at a place where they will have the opportunities to build skill. While the opportunities created today at the bottom of the pyramid are still valuable, these are not the kind of opportunities that will move the social standing of unskilled workers and give them the means to create more and better opportunities. I believe that societies make progress not by pulling people along, but by giving people at every level the means to move up. Gig work is not a solution for skilling, for sure, but it provides the economic opportunity to earn more than what unskilled workers (and in some cases even skilled workers like plumbers and electricians) earn. The onus of utilizing the increased economic opportunity still stays with the worker and their attitude towards progress. If a gig worker returns to their village after making quick money via gig work, they are unlikely to have made meaningful progress in upskilling. If the companies that operate in the gig work paradigm try to become exploitative then this economic upside will go away and the system won't work either.

Outside of the government, the role of providing opportunities for upward mobility for the unskilled has traditionally been that of the manufacturing or services sector—mainly the manufacturing sector in India. Over the last decade and a half of the start-up boom, gig work and supply chain work have added to that mix. From the millions of riders delivering e-commerce and food orders to the trained technicians and beauty professionals zipping around our cities—these are the kinds of jobs that didn't exist ten years ago so it would have been impossible for many of them to dream of having access to this form of employment. The reality, though, is that it is still not enough. The kind of boost, incentives and focus that go into sectors like construction, infrastructure or manufacturing have failed to generate the type of service employment that would provide the opportunity for upward economic mobility to large sections of society (like what the automobile and petroleum industries and industrialized farming did for America after the Second World War).

At the same time, the criss-cross of working in complex on-ground situations with different boundary lines of politics, regulation, and law and order, have deterred many people from building businesses that require a large on-ground presence. We need a hundred-fold increase in the kind of stories that lead from garages to factory buildings. This is important because there is still a deep imbalance in opportunities that are available for everyone. These imbalances might be a result of millennia of discrimination, but they exist—and they are likely the largest drag on our economic development. Entrepreneurs in this country should feel confident about building labour-intensive businesses and willingly provide more avenues for investing in the productivity of their workers.

A society that is not set up to make its workers more productive by facilitating their work is going to find it hard to maintain economic progress by just pushing people hard. This is a big lesson for companies that want to grow into large organizations—the ability to do that encompasses making the right choices today. You have to either figure out how to demonstrably create more economic opportunity and also invest in upskilling and mobilizing people, like the outsourcing sector was able to do with the white-collar workforce, or become technologically proficient at operating massive gig systems to side-step the issues. Solutions that are dependent on better delivery of services, including education, healthcare and access to quality of life by the public sector, are still not within view, and if available, are likely not accessible to the target workforce.

So while we are now a more capitalistic society, we need to be relentless towards opportunity creation for economic development. The hundreds of bright young people who man our shop floors or deliver your orders need to view this work as a stepping stone to even more opportunities with their own career path and development. It is only in the last few years that entrepreneurship has started to be accepted in the privileged sections of society outside of the business class. Earlier, there were some people who were supposed to do business who did business. If you didn't belong to that group, you found a job. Now compare the privilege that we, as English-speaking people in the country, have over someone who has never thought of a job or business beyond daily labour.

The mental model shift is enormous, and we have not even started seeing the effects of it. While our richer classes have accepted capitalism in all its forms—it is an acceptable profession to have your own business—the not-so-rich classes are yet to look beyond the security of government jobs. This is why every time there is an exam for police jobs in Tau Devilal Stadium in Gurgaon, there is a line of over a thousand applicants for fifty seats, but every single business looking for semi-skilled or dependable unskilled labour is struggling to find people willing to even learn.

For organizations, gig work has helped overcome a lack of trust, and for the gig workers, it has helped them deal with the unpredictability of their life in a better way. The unfortunate reality about trust at the bottom of the pyramid is that a society or a business community where everyone is viewed with suspicion or distrust is not a healthy growth environment for the ecosystem. It introduces friction for businesses to scale up and that, in turn, creates fewer opportunities for the folks who stand to gain the most from the impact that these businesses can have.

It is not an easy thing to solve—it is the outcome of years of lack of accountability, discrimination and the triumph of influence over justice for a very long time. Most of the incoming workforce at the bottom of the pyramid is already attuned to this reality.

A large section of people who are moving into formal employment from agriculture (where minimum wage is hardly ever met) or other completely unorganized sectors look at everything around them with an even higher level of suspicion. Not only do they lack trust in the different arms of the government (like law enforcement) and the private sector, they also don't trust anyone who doesn't look, talk or think like them. This is the reason why delivery partners at our first station hung out with people from their own states. As unfortunate as that is, it is the reality of operating businesses in India which interface closely with a workforce that is moving into the formal economy at the entry level. This is the layer that has so far not experienced formal employment or even opportunities that can let them earn more than the basic income. The moment we move to workers beyond the top 20 per cent of earners in the current working population in the country, we'll find that all those coming into the unskilled sectors have had no experience with formal employment. One of the biggest things gig work has been able to deliver for them is the opportunity to earn more, unburdened by the legacy of social issues, informal employment or lack of access and education.

In summary, there is a long road ahead to building trust across societal lines—and somewhere the presence of the gig economy has taken away the need to try to change that, making the relationship transactional. It is a new-world solution to a problem that has existed for a while, and something that was not possible before the advent of mobile phones and cheap data. Whether or not it will lead to a continuously upskilling workforce is unknown, but it has provided an operating model for large-scale earning opportunities for the workforce and a more predictable way of getting them to do the work that employers expected.

Gig work in our context and place as a country has helped break the vicious cycle of lack of trust and economic opportunity at the bottom of the pyramid. It has certainly created opportunities that regular employment could not create, due to the way employers are viewed in our society. A number of companies could start as small shops and go on to become large enterprises because they could overcome the unpredictability of the employee work ethic by utilizing technology and a gig-based contract with the workers. This is something that will continue to show up in more segments of the work that is done in India as economic development shoots ahead of social development, leading to the adoption of a more trust-based system of work. For companies, though, my learning from having to build with an unskilled workforce was that thinking deeply about adopting gig work should also come from a deeper understanding of the needs of the business, the economic ability of the business to pay and a commitment from the organization to build technology. If companies choose to operate in a zero-trust system then almost every part of the system will need to operate flawlessly and with transparency.

In 2018, I was waiting for my burger at the Burger Singh outlet on Golf Course Road in Gurgaon late at night when I was approached by one of the delivery personnel waiting there. He was one of the folks who had been in the room that day in 2014 when I was making my impassioned plea to delivery partners, and I even managed to remember his name: Pathak (unsure if he will read this book). He was waiting to pick up an order from the restaurant for one of the food-delivery platforms. I greeted him and asked how he was doing. He was in good spirits and happy to see me—he had seen the company grow from the outside and happily told me that he bragged about the fact that he had worked at the company in its early days to those around him. I, however, felt sad. Here was someone who had worked with us in the early days. Unlike a lot of early employees who had started off in entry-level roles and grown with the company, gaining both skills and a better life (and shares in the company), here was a person who had left the journey simply because he didn't trust in the vision of anyone who was like me (not famous or on the front pages of newspapers). He could potentially have been in a very different place in life both monetarily and professionally if he had trusted our little company's future. He had missed out on an opportunity to be a beneficiary of our company's success till that time. Instead, he was still doing the same job even after four years. I felt that while individual choices do matter, somewhere our systems fail at allowing people to access the information and trust which help them make better choices.

Pathak, for his part, was way more optimistic. He told me about his new bike, which was an inside joke, since, back in the day, his bike would constantly break down (and we used to think it was an excuse). He was clearly happy doing what he was doing and likely earning more than what the market paid for a job at his skill level. Yes, he had missed out on a different life of learning more things and adding skills, but gig work provided him a way to earn more by working harder, which was a trade-off he was willing to take. He talked about how gig work was the only job which did not induce anxiety in him—he felt he had more control over his life. If something unknown came up (which in life always does), he knew that he could earn later during the day or on another day. The burden of an unpredictable life didn't mean he would lose his job—gig work provided him the flexibility to deal with that. For someone who might have responsibilities as the go-to person for their family, relatives or community, the flexibility that gig work provided was more valuable than the stability of a job. This was a new paradigm for folks who knew that they couldn't get traditional jobs or be able to hold onto them. Earning via gig work seemed to be a lifestyle choice for Pathak and millions of others like him.

Over the first year, after we had started off by delivering for just a few local shops, we grew our network to almost three hundred stores. This included regional and national chains of supermarkets and grocery stores that used our service to deliver to their customers. By the end of the year, we had raised our first round of capital from Sequoia Capital (now Peak XV) and Deepi to expand the business. We had also started investing in our technology systems, and in December of 2014 we launched the Grofers app for consumers, where they could place their orders directly with the shops instead of calling them or sending them a WhatsApp message. This app was scaling rapidly and was a major focus for us at the end of the year.

As our first year of operation was ending, we were on the cusp of introducing a few changes that would make us confront the realities of yet another big piece of building in India—trying to provide capital to the business. The lessons of trust and predictability were about to show up again in how we tried to fund and sustain our fledgling business.

2015

GAMBLING AND CAPITAL

In November 2015, we found ourselves sitting in the main conference room at the Grofers office in Gurgaon at 8 a.m. We had just celebrated raising $120 million in capital for Grofers in the same conference room two days ago. But that day our body language was in sharp contrast—with grim faces all around, it looked like everyone was dealing with the shock in their own way. I had been woken up by Rishi the previous night because a member of the service staff employed in one of our city warehouses had been found dead by the side of a road, their throat slit.

The police had approached us for details, and we were trying to figure out what had happened. Other than that the deceased had signed out of our facility in the evening and about eight hours later their body was found in some bushes close to Faridabad, we had very limited information. The person was the employee of a company that provided cleaning services at our facilities and was carrying an entry card for the same facility. The police had therefore approached us to get details on their movements. The situation was made more tense because only a few days before that, some of the delivery partners in a nearby facility had ganged up and beaten one of our store managers. This had led to a crackdown on the erring partners and we had fired a number of people. The same people were protesting outside the facility in question, and we were left wondering whether the two events were related. Deep inside, I felt it was a bridge too far. No one in their right mind would resort to murder to send a message like this.

Till that time, we had experienced a few unfortunate incidents that tend to happen when you have a large on-ground personnel presence. One of our 4,000 employees at the time had died of a cardiac arrest a few months ago, but this was different—this was murder. It was a brutal shock to our sensibilities to have this happen so close to us. In the midst of all this, we had other challenges to overcome as well, which put our focus back on figuring out how the unfortunate incident affected our organization and the thousands who were dependent on it.

Not only were we trying to provide the details that we could to law enforcement and our employees, but we were also debating whether this information needed to be passed along to our existing and future investors, and when. We were still relatively new to the overall ecosystem of raising capital and were unsure if something like this would raise red flags and if investors would not want to invest in a company that had such exposure to on-ground realities. At that time, though, the consequences were a faraway thought—we were waiting for details on what had actually happened.

The police were reluctant to share any more information than was absolutely necessary, so we could also relay only so much to our employees and investors, even if we wanted to. We waited for most of the day for any new information and finally decided that we would give our potential investors a summary of the ongoing event and whatever information we had till then. That evening we called up each of the new and existing investors individually, and let them know what we were dealing with.

To our surprise, our investors had seen some version of these kinds of crises in other businesses like ours. They had been investors in companies like Flipkart, Ola and numerous other operationally intensive businesses in India, and also in other countries, and knew that, no matter how brutal, unfortunate surprises were part and parcel of everyday life. Not only were they understanding of how stressed we were but they also offered to connect us with other founders and businesses who had dealt with these things in the past. In fact, talking to some of the other people in the ecosystem who had navigated similar challenges calmed us enough to start getting our focus back on the business.

For a few days, though, the dichotomy of where we were—raising a massive round of capital for our business, and the ground reality of operating this business every day in a populated, messy and unorganized environment—was the biggest thing on my mind. This was not something new for us, just that, at that moment, it felt like the stakes were much higher—both in the grim reality of what had happened and how far we had come.

Back in 2014, we had picked up more than a few of our employees from scenes of accidents or been forced to stop business in a certain market due to the local strongmen. None of these, however, had seemed like things that could derail the future of the company. This time, it was different.

We really needed to raise this capital so that everything we had built to that point, including the hopes and dreams of hundreds of folks in office and thousands of personnel on the ground, could continue flourishing. The fate of our organization was very vulnerable to whether we could or could not get capital. It felt like the brutal incident might put our future at risk.

This, however, was not the first time that our organization was facing this reality of being in a tough spot and needing some kind of financing, nor would it be the last—this was just the grimmest episode. Our desperate need to seek capital started way before 2015. For the reader to understand how we started on this journey of raising capital, let me also give some context on how the business had progressed over the first two years of its existence.

Back in 2014, when our business had started working with local shops to provide them with a common delivery service, we realized that one of the more interesting aspects of this business was managing cash-on-delivery orders for some shops that delivered to customers. While a number of our clients were distributors delivering their products in small quantities to local shops, we were getting more and more shops to make home deliveries through us, particularly grocery stores and pharmacies. Even in 2015, 83 per cent of customers of e-commerce used to avail cash on delivery instead of paying online.[1] For offline stores, this number was 100 per cent before the advent of Unified Payments Interface (UPI). Customers would call the shop or WhatsApp them their orders, and the shopkeeper would punch the delivery address and the amount to be collected for the goods into our system.

Invariably, we would end up collecting a lot of cash from these orders, and since our delivery partners were the ones collecting the cash, we had to find a way to send this money to the shops without the delivery partner doing a reverse trip to the pick-up shop. Making another delivery would be a more productive use of that time. We started collecting the cash from customers, depositing it in our accounts at the end of each day and then transferring it to the local merchants. Everyone knows that cash reigns supreme in the Indian economy but how deep and impactful the cash systems are can only be understood when you see the actual nature of the cash economy.

By depositing the cash through our bank, we got a significant advantage in solving a hard problem—that of providing change to customers at their doorstep. Our delivery partners had to provide change to customers at their doorstep on behalf of the shops for whom we delivered. This was a big problem at the time. In 2014, before UPI and mobile wallets proliferated, getting change for ₹100 in the local market meant you had to pay anywhere between ₹105 and ₹110. Change was selling at a premium to the actual value of the cash. Most small businesses had to arrange for small bank notes from the grey market to be able to give change to customers for home deliveries. This was an unseen cost of doing business for them. The problem was so big that the premium on small bank notes used to sometimes climb as high as 20 per cent. In 2014–15, there was a high demand–supply mismatch for bank notes and coins, with demand exceeding supply by nearly 6 billion pieces for coins alone.[2]

Most banks were not able to provide that much change except to customers who did regular and big business with them. By handling the cash for our merchants as well, we were able to manage this adhoc cash requirement for small change for our delivery partners to some extent, but it was a perpetual high-wire act of preserving small change and depositing large bank notes. Doing this repeatedly though, was a small edge we had in the operational segment of the business, because we could reuse a single source of small change among multiple stores. For instance, if we handled cash deliveries for a hundred stores, we had access to a larger variety of notes than we did for a single store. As a result, we could aggregate and distribute this small change more efficiently across the network. Additionally, handling payments and relieving our clients of the accompanying problem of providing change was also a valued enough service in the market, which led to us signing up more shops thick and fast.

SK and I counting cash collected from deliveries at the end of a long day

On a hot summer day, SK and I stood outside the branch of one of the largest banks in the country. The bank's security guard was a little hesitant to let us in. This was because our shirts were covered in sweat and we were wearing arm sleeves that had fake tattoos on them. We were only wearing the sleeves to protect our arms because the summer sun in Gurgaon was ruthless if you were out riding a motorcycle for a whole day—which was what we had been doing (motorcycles were the only sensible way to move between markets and find reliable parking).

We had not yet raised external capital for our business and were operating on earned revenue and investment from personal savings. The business was getting bigger every week, but we were facing new challenges, most of which required us to have more money in the bank. Our collective savings were not enough to support the business. I had a lot of belief that we had stumbled onto something that had myriad potential. But in the day-to-day grind of being out in the hot summer sun, hustling to find the next set of customers, the lack of money in the bank and the everyday frustrations from rejections in the sales cycles were like sensitive wounds that flared up whenever something did not go our way.

Our frequent visits to the banks to deposit cash and the growing scale of our business also meant we were becoming increasingly well known in the local bank branch. They got to know about our business from the little banter SK or I would have while depositing the cash (SK often carried a few lakhs in currency notes in his backpack to deposit at the end of the day). The collecting, accounting, distribution and depositing of the cash used to take so much of our time every day that we even briefly considered building a technology product just to solve this problem for the broader market. There was an ill-conceived 'I owe you' card for change that we tried to get our client shops to use, but advent of UPI made this problem almost redundant and, thankfully, we stuck to doing deliveries.

Despite all of this money flowing through the business, we were still a small and upcoming enterprise, barely a few months old. We had an urgent requirement to inject more capital into our business.

We had recently signed a contract with the grocery chain Le Marche—as our first large customer in Delhi-NCR. We were able to prove to Le Marche that we could meet their delivery needs and soon got business from all their outlets in the city, and they requested us to start some deliveries for them that were farther away from their stores.

This new business opportunity required us to invest in a four-wheeler cargo van and this was why we were now entering this large bank—for a loan to help grow our business. This was the first time we had felt the need to look for capital outside of whatever SK and I had invested from our savings into the company to start the operations a few months earlier.

We did a lot of research online on whether we could get a loan from a bank to get a cargo van and our hopes were low. There was a lot of marketing by banks about giving loans to small businesses but very little detail on what kind of businesses did or did not get loans—those decisions operated on qualitative criteria that you had to visit the bank to find out. There were no real organized Non-Banking Financial Company (NBFC) options for early-stage companies like ours at the time either, so the banks remained our best bet.

Our cash flow and revenue every month was enough to cover the cost of the estimated EMI of a cargo van, but we didn't have the bank balance in our company account to invest in a van. If we spent the money from our personal accounts, it would severely dent our ability to run our households for a longer time. We figured, with the bleak hope that our credentials as engineering graduates who had a great track record of working in big companies would account for something, that it was worth a shot to try and get a loan for ₹4,50,000 that would help us earn more revenue and grow the business. We could pay for roughly 25 per cent of the cost of the vehicle but the loan amount was needed to cover the rest. We had also hoped that the people at the bank, who were seeing us grow every day and depositing ever-increasing amounts of cash would be able to offer us a solution.

Needless to say, our hopes were dashed rather quickly. Even though we were carrying almost the same amount of cash to deposit in the bank from our collections every day as the amount we required for a loan, we were told that there were certain criteria for businesses to get loans and we didn't fulfil any of them—particularly that our business wasn't even two years old and we had never actually submitted any financials to the Ministry of Corporate Affairs (MCA) website. The fundamentals of the business or the cash flows, or most metrics around health and scalability of the business that I had learnt over the years, didn't seem to matter.

This was a sobering reminder that credit in the Indian ecosystem is hard to come by. This was way more acute at that time than it would be ten years later, but it is still largely true. There are two reasons for this, as we learnt over the years.

The first one was borne out by our experiences and learnings from working with a lot of small businesses who had to raise capital, usually from informal sources at exorbitant interest rates because the formal market was closed for them. Prior to Goods and Services Tax (GST) days, businesses with formal and reliable income statements and balance sheets were few, especially in the local markets. Almost 93 per cent of the Medium and Small Enterprises (MSME) sector was unregistered in 2013–14.[3] In the absence of a proven repository of reliable financials, the banks could not extend any credit to these enterprises. It took small shops and small businesses a very long time to reach the point where banks were willing to offer them growth loans (loans to grow the business). It happened late in the business's life cycle, when they had reached a certain volume of business/revenue/scale. Even then, a personal connection at the bank was usually the way to go—a practice that has caused large-scale issues in the Indian banking system. The banking scandals involving large loan sums and fugitive businessmen are more commonly known versions of this problem. This is corruption in a different form—you get close to someone at the bank who can help with the approval process and they take a cut to give you a loan. Of course, the folks who end up asking for these loans have already indicated that they are willing to bend the law and are more than happy to indulge in other practices, like siphoning off the loan or not repaying it at all. This isn't just a phenomenon that you see in the big defaults that make the headlines, but an everyday occurrence all over the country.

The underlying reason that the formal route is so difficult is due to the high default rates caused by these bad actors in the local economies.[4] These folks know that enforcement of penalties is nearly impossible, so they get loans approved with no intention of repaying them. For context, the amount owed by wilful defaulters to Indian banks was ₹23,000 crore in 2012. By 2022, this had jumped ten times to ₹2.4 lakh crore.[5] The resultant impact of this on grassroots entrepreneurship is debilitating as the processes to curb these default rates also end up stifling reasonable terms of credit to honest businesses. In trying to stop small-scale defaults by bad actors, our formal credit system ends up leaving out the good businesses. There are systemic needs in the early stage of business that credit as a source of capital is best placed to serve—things like working capital, payroll advances, capital expenditures or even submitting regulatory dues like taxes.

The credit ecosystem excludes new companies from this source of capital almost completely. The result is that the credit needs end up getting fulfilled by unorganized or even exploitative sources of capital.

Late in 2015, when we were starting our business of delivering fruits and vegetables to customers, I ended up spending a lot of time in local vegetable mandis like Khandsa in Haryana and Azadpur in Delhi. At the mandis, we met with different market operators who played varied roles in keeping the supply chain of fruits and vegetables humming so that the produce reached our stores and also the doorsteps of customers. Some of them were specialists in supply chain, some were specialists in particular kinds of goods and some were providing the capital that allowed farmers to get paid early. While we realized that this was an ecosystem that was absolutely necessary in a developing market, we also recognized that the inefficiency of the credit markets meant that the added costs were enormous.

A pushcart vendor who sold fruits and vegetables by going around a locality all day was one of the cases that brought out the real cost of capital. The equation on the ground was pretty simple. The pushcart vendor would come to the local market every morning and would get ₹1,000 worth of vegetables or fruits (whatever they were selling) on credit. In 2015, the standard in Gurgaon was that the vendor had to pay ₹1,100 at the end of the day. In simple terms, the cost of credit for the pushcart vendor was 10 per cent per day or 3650 per cent per year on simple interest alone. In contrast, anyone reading this book is likely to get a home loan at around 10 per cent per year. This was before accounting for the mark-up at which they were selling the produce in the first place. What the vendor had to earn for themselves was over and above the ₹1,100 they had to return to be able to get more supply for the following day. This was the credit system available to the entry-level entrepreneur. The chain then goes up. The wholesaler giving the products to the vendor was also sometimes borrowing at exorbitant rates to give the products down the line.

This interest rate goes down as the scale and formalization of business goes up, but over the years, the expectation has been that there would be credit available to small businesses or entrepreneurs at a significantly higher interest rate; the vegetable market was just a microcosm of this environment. The fact that only 16 per cent of the credit demand of MSMEs in 2017 was met through formal financing is proof that our credit system for emerging companies is not helpful.[6] The remaining need is often met through informal sources of credit like moneylenders, chit funds and friends or family. These sources charge anywhere between 30–60 per cent interest for these needs.

These interest costs reflect in the prices that get charged to end customers since the risk and the interest have to be paid by the intermediary business. Emerging businesses, therefore, start off uncompetitive on prices of their goods and services, and start cutting corners to become competitive. Not charging taxes like GST, employing a labour force below minimum wage and not complying with any quality standards become necessary steps to save money and make their service competitive.

Even for us, this lack of capital continued to be frustrating for quite some time. During the period when we were trying to borrow money for a van, our business was doubling or tripling in size every month. We were struggling to invest meaningfully in the business as we didn't generate enough profit, so very often we were borrowing from our own bank accounts or asking our friends or my wife for money, so we could tide over working capital challenges. We also had to cut corners. For a while, we were ferrying around our cargo in a second-hand Maruti 800 that was way past its prime. Since it was not meant to handle cargo, we would often also end up damaging the products we were transporting.

We wanted to be focused on adding more merchants, building out our tech and not be hassled about tiding over a cash crunch every two weeks. After the third continuous month of borrowing money for working capital, we eventually started seriously considering talking to strategic investors and venture capital firms to raise capital by selling some equity in the company. It was a route that we had been ignoring until then because it seemed like a lengthy process that would take our focus away from the business. What we needed at the time was short-term credit, which would have helped us along as a business, but now we were turning to capital sources that are traditionally much more expensive and, though we didn't know it at the time, these capital sources were not looking to invest in businesses that wanted to use their investment as working capital or for buying fixed assets, such as cargo vans, since neither would generate a measurable return on their investment. Our experience in raising private capital would be the second learning about the lack of capital in the Indian ecosystem.

The first few private venture investors who approached us were not particularly sold on the business model. This was part of the reason that we had not explored venture capital as a potential source of funding very seriously till that point. There was a general reluctance from venture firms to invest in operationally involved businesses in India, and rightfully so. Operations required building out physical infrastructure for low-margin businesses and if there were opportunities to invest in asset-light businesses at the time, that would be preferred. Venture investing or investing in new businesses for equity was a relatively nascent but growing sector in the middle of the last decade. India had a few investment firms which were willing to invest in high-risk technology ventures. Outside of Infoedge (the parent of Naukri.com), there were no large companies investing from their balance sheet either. As a result, only about 20 per cent of the venture and private equity funding in India in 2015 went towards asset-heavy sectors.[7]

Venture investing in itself is a risky business globally. Some of the most successful venture firms will invest in hundreds of companies, of which only a few (maybe only a couple) will become massive and deliver enough gains to make up for the loss incurred by investing in hundreds of others. Therefore, for venture investing to thrive in India, there has to be an opportunity to build at least a few extremely large businesses—without which the venture model would not work. Digital businesses, like Google or Facebook, can become extremely large over small periods of time with relatively low investment in physical infrastructure (which, by definition, takes time to create). So, for venture investing, this is the most preferred type of business, one that requires nearly no physical touchpoints or infrastructure. Physical infrastructure needs time to build, operationalize, scale and turn into a profitable machine. It also cannot scale non-linearly like digital businesses can. Therefore, for outsized return, it is better for venture firms to chase digital-only businesses that can scale with the click of a button and by adding a server.

However, the Indian market at the time was in a bigger need for businesses to invest in physical infrastructure than just digital-only plays. With the overall infrastructure and market development lagging behind Western economies, any technology business that was trying to do the same in India had to likely build out parts of the infrastructure as well. Almost all the large companies from the early 2010s that have come up were built on large offline elements—whether it was Flipkart, Zomato, Policy

Bazaar or Delhivery. These companies had to invest in physical infrastructure in different forms, and not just rely on digital scale. The reason these businesses were able to attract capital despite the physical component was that they were in spaces that were desirable and sizeable in opportunity, and there was a possibility that they could become extremely large, which they did.

Digital-only businesses in India started making a run much later in the decade and their ability to truly build scale in large numbers is still a few years out. Outside of stock-broking apps like Zerodha or payment platforms on UPI, there have not been any businesses that did not need physical touchpoints. This meant that back in 2014, the nascent venture ecosystem was forced to invest in businesses with physical touchpoints due to a lack of options. The success of Flipkart and Snapdeal had given birth to a number of businesses that were building out e-commerce or physically involved businesses, and we were just one of them. The space was competitive and capital was limited.

Despite our initial hesitation to approach venture capital firms, we realized that there was some appetite and we would have to raise the capital in a competitive environment. We weren't looking for a lot of capital by the standards of the day and the initial money was relatively easier to find—although it didn't seem like that at the time.

After starting our efforts to raise private capital in 2014, we met with multiple investors, even got an offer for funding which was not honoured and somehow managed, towards the end of the year, to raise ₹3 crore from Deepi and Sequoia Capital. We had been looking for outside capital for our small business for months and the fruit of that effort was getting an offer from early-stage venture investors. This struggle to raise capital, though, did not prepare us for the rollercoaster ride we were about to embark on in 2015.

In December 2014, we launched the Grofers consumer app. The app aggregated all the stores that we were delivering for, and gave the customers a view of all the products that each store sold. This was an extension of our delivery business for the shops that got orders on the phone or WhatsApp and used Grofers for delivery. Now, in addition to that, we were able to get more orders for these shops via our app and deliver for them as well. This venture was better for us and better for the shops since it also generated new business, which all shops wanted, and we could earn higher commissions than what we would get for purely doing deliveries. Grocery shops were the largest segment that got orders in this business because we could not list the pharmacy-related products due to unclear regulations.

The app really took off. It was a service that customers greatly needed—fast delivery of products. By the middle of 2015, Grofers was in rapid expansion mode on all fronts—customers, team size and geographies. We had recently launched Bangalore (now Bengaluru) and Mumbai operations as well and were struggling to keep up with execution, not to mention that we were piling up losses. Over a six-month period, we had gone from a business with steady revenue from shops and slight profitability to a rapidly expanding one, growing 20–30 per cent every single week. This meant we had to hire people quickly, make up for the lack of systems with even more people and, at the same time, invest in building the systems. We weren't the only ones either. There were many other companies doing exactly what we were doing and piling up losses in order to get a foothold in the new segment of rapid grocery delivery.

With a number of companies chasing each other to stand out for the customer, the need for capital was high among all of them. In a now-familiar cycle, the only way to succeed at this and catch the eye of the venture investing community was to be even more aggressive. Traction—the pace at which a nascent business grows—is the name of the game when unproven business models are looking for risk capital. As a result, a number of companies in the space, including us, were now spending money quickly to showcase traction and, equally quickly, joining the queue of companies looking for more capital to show more traction. It was a heady and dizzying phase of taking losses to grow faster and raise more money to be able to take more losses.

We initially thought that finding a strategic investor for our business would be a better bet in the face of tremendous competition, and we were working with enough large retail businesses to be a valuable partner to at least one of them. Accumulating losses to support a growing business, however, did not fit into the way of building businesses that almost everyone in the Indian ecosystem subscribed to. This was the period where companies like Zomato and Flipkart were panned in the media for expanding even though they were loss-making businesses. I remember explaining to fairly senior people at a conglomerate in Mumbai that app-based consumer businesses did not grow neighbourhood by neighbourhood. We had to build large-scale infrastructure, invest in technology and scale well ahead of time and only then would we able to amortize these costs as the scale of the business grew. This holds as true today as it did in 2014 and 2015. And as with Indian businesses in 2015, the ability and willingness of businesses to invest in future technology and growth still remains limited.

The reason for this is that the public markets tend to punish any significant investment in loss-making ventures and that meant almost negligible investment levels from the top fifty listed companies in India into future businesses, except where it was their primary business. The willingness to accept that a dedicated team will have a better shot at disrupting an industry with technology than the known ways of building large businesses in India was—and still is—extremely low. The concept of disruption is lost on large businesses who have always seen their scale and access as a moat in the Indian ecosystem. Even though, by the middle of 2015, we were delivering from stores owned by some of the largest conglomerates in the country (we used to get them orders from customers through the Grofers app), there was zero interest from them in owning a part of our business as an investment in the future. Either the conglomerates wanted to own the entire business (preferably by paying a nominal amount because we were loss-making) or they had a view (which almost all of them have to this day) that they could just replicate the business model by outsourcing technology development to a service provider.

A number of large businesses had some of these principles related to risk aversion ingrained in their way of operating and these mindsets were hard to overcome. Large companies in India knew that the safer way of doing business was to collaborate with a proven partner from abroad (proven technology and a partner from a developed country also meant limited meddling from the government in the business), rather than bet on a few kids with a no-name business in Gurgaon. No one was putting up money for research and development, neither then nor now. Case in point, even our large and successful pharma sector is mostly a generic medicine production machine and not a new-drug development industry.

The 'profit today over investing today and profit tomorrow' way of thinking was widely the cause for a lot of incumbents having trouble understanding why there were so many loss-making start-ups getting hyped and raising capital. After a few months of trying to get strategic investment in our business from many large consumer retail chains in India, we gave up on this avenue of raising capital altogether. We had realized that the investment in future profit and disruption was still coming from venture capital firms and not conglomerates. Venture capital was an expensive source of capital and not as patient as was needed for businesses like ours, but that is what was available. When I say venture capital is expensive, it is due to the fact that the equivalent 'return rate' expectation from a venture capital invested dollar is much higher than any other source of capital. As a demonstration, if a company gets credit at an interest rate of 12 per cent then it is probably paying the equivalent of 25 per cent or more for venture capital—because of the underlying risk that must be factored in. Practically, it doesn't work like that, but it is a way to think about the cost of raising venture capital.

As our consumer app started getting attention from customers, it began to see a lot of traction from the venture investing community. Two large events at the time were powering this interest—the first was the rapid rise of Flipkart, which had raised successive rounds of capital from international investors. The company had cumulatively raised $2.6 billion across four funding rounds in 2014 and 2015.[8] The investors could see an Amazon for India potentially rising here and that generated a lot of interest in look-alike businesses or those that were ancillary to e-commerce—hyperlocal deliveries was one of them. The second event was the proliferation of smartphones, which meant a lot of convenience-providing mobile app-based businesses were coming up in the American market.[9] Primary among them at the time were grocery- and food-delivery apps like Instacart, Postmates and Doordash. Investors with exposure to those markets soon came looking for look-alike businesses in India as well, and companies like Grofers fit the bill.

Early on, almost all the interest we were getting was from international investors. This was a time when there were around fifty-four grocery-delivery start-ups in Delhi-NCR alone. Capital was starting to flow to the sector and the success of Flipkart, Snapdeal and many others was not lost on young, educated and ambitious entrepreneurs who, like us, understood how to build technology. With a growing business and some good execution, we were also able to attract a lot of capital quickly. In fact, it was not just us—there was a lot of capital influx in India to back early-stage companies.

It was in 2015 that the Indian markets saw the first real deluge of private venture capital, all of it foreign, poured into nascent technology-led ventures.[10] In the years prior, Flipkart had been the vanguard of raising capital and had attracted a lot of money really quickly, followed by Snapdeal also doing the same. Other companies like Zomato and Policy Bazaar were becoming household names but had not raised as much capital—2015 was different though. Young ventures, even a few months old, were attracting seed rounds of $5 million and $10 million. At the time, we were a nearly-two-year-old business and raising early-stage rounds in the beginning felt odd. We were competing for capital with businesses that were still just getting off the ground and some that were just ideas on paper. In hindsight, because we were an operating business for over two years, we were able to move through the stages of fundraising quickly. Within a twelve-month period, we went from having raised no capital to raising $165 million in total. A majority of this came in the funding round led by SoftBank (the Japanese telecom conglomerate known most famously for its leader Masayoshi Son's aggressive bets) in November 2015.

Private funding deals—albeit among only a handful of companies mostly operated by technologists—were becoming front-page news and for the first time, it felt like our start-up was really taking off. For a while, it looked like we were going to be playing the dangerous game of scaling up, increasing losses, raising capital, scaling up further, and so on, endlessly. The look-alike businesses in the West, because of which we had got our initial cheques from venture capitalists, were growing larger. This seemed to give a lot of confidence that 'X for India' would also become huge. There wasn't a dramatic understanding of the Indian ecosystem that was powering this belief, at least in my view—just that something would get built. Ironically, it worked, as something did eventually get built, albeit in a different form.

The rush to scale up the business meant that we were also chasing the boom cycle and raising capital while our losses were piling up. Nor were we the only ones. Everyone's place in the space was becoming more precarious as they were risking sitting on higher losses to showcase more growth to be able to raise more capital.

Just like all boom cycles, a few months later, the boom cycle of 2015 also ended. While Grofers became a poster child for the excess of the period to some, that is, a company attracting too much capital too soon, we felt extremely lucky that we had the capital to invest in the business and were sure that we would use the capital responsibly—investing in the long-term health of the business. In our world view at the time, the money in the bank gave us the runway to do things the right way, improve customer experience, build long-term infrastructure and not spend money on deals and discounts just to scale.

Customers were liking the fast delivery that we provided and we were excited to make the business larger. As the funding in the ecosystem dried up, the number of companies shutting shop started rising. The doom and gloom around sectors that were considered unstoppable a few months earlier became a lot more palpable. I naively thought that we had survived the manic contest of burn-grow-raise-burn and the shutdowns were a validation that we were the best company to come out of it.

While we were still better off, a number of companies became victims of not having enough capital or of competing too heavily by ballooning their losses excessively, to the point of shutting down within months. Through most of 2016, we saw a lot of companies that we knew well go down due to their inability to raise more capital. For the first time, it felt like the free market forces of capital allocation were operating in a very small part of the Indian economy—early-stage technology investing. The boom cycle lasted less than a year but the resulting downcycle, lower investment activity in early-stage businesses and contraction of existing businesses, carried on for a longer period of time. This period also showed us the different aspects from this boom time and how raising capital from venture investors wasn't a straight line to success.

Today, when I see eager-eyed founders pitching on TV shows or a number of people who consider raising venture capital as the de facto model of funding a business, I see the same naivete with which we were trying to operate. There are multiple ways to build a business, over multiple time periods in many sectors. For each scenario, the kind of capital required is different. Not every business out there is meant to be funded by venture capital—just like every business cannot take on debt. The reality of taking on high-risk capital is that it works well if the business and its founders are okay to keep doubling down on the risk and, more important, that is what the business needs. More often than not, it means you are in a fast-growing disruptive space where technology is the moat. This also means that good execution and excellence in decision-making are table stakes and not differentiators. It becomes a high-stakes gamble—the probability of success or survival increasingly depends on external factors, such as the overall funding environments and the level of investor interest in a particular sector, rather than just the quality of execution or the founder' decisions. Of course, exceptions exist to every scenario, but broadly the kinds of businesses venture capital backs are inherently high-risk, meaning most do not succeed and only a small fraction achieve exceptionally high returns. I see a lot of folks who want to start businesses and even join high-growth businesses after having spent most of their time in stable careers. They rightfully believe in their capabilities and want to believe that success in the world of start-ups, especially those funded by venture capital, is largely meritocratic. And, yes, while access is meritocratic for the most part, success is a bigger gamble than people think. Raising capital is not a goal in itself and doesn't guarantee anything. When entrepreneurs bring in an external investor, especially a venture capital firm, whose expectations of success are in multiples of their investment, and the success rate is really low, they are just starting the journey of high-risk bets. This is something that was not apparent to me when we started. The success in this scenario has to come from multiple high-risk bets, not just one of starting up. Additionally, when we were involved in a high-stakes race to scale up and increase losses, we didn't stop to think of how we were going to get out of the pattern when the funding cycles went bust. This happened not only to us but to a lot of other companies at the time as well.

The very public success stories of companies and founders raising large rounds or even taking the companies public mask the real risk reward here. Just like venture capital firms have low success rates in their bets, the companies that they fund also have low success rates. The chances of success are closer to that of winning a lottery than they are to a coin toss. When I moved back to India, I did not appreciate that I was taking a high-risk gamble. If I succeeded, the success would be much bigger than what I could potentially hope for in the corporate world abroad. However, the outcome of failure would obviously be much worse.

It is human nature to think that the odds of our own success are better than they are. For businesses too, the same skewed ratio of compulsive gambling exists. It isn't enough if you win one hand of blackjack. In the world of venture capital, you have to turn right around and keep hitting till you win everything or go bust, even in the very next hand.

Contrary to the norms of operating in this environment, we had chosen to go conservative and use the capital to build systems and plug loopholes in our operations and customer experience. We had also decided to pivot our business to something else. Unfortunately, the reason for both our problems—high losses and stagnation in growth—was the same. We were extremely reliant on the local supply chain of stores and distributors, which was highly fragmented and, therefore, unreliable for a business of scale. As we were growing bigger, we were also increasingly incurring losses. In the face of this, we decided to move to next-day delivery in a bid to control losses. We were trying to live another day.

For our investors, however, it was a sign that either we were not willing to go big for glory or that they had misinterpreted the opportunity or the team. When we started talking about slowing down and fixing things that were broken, a few of them wanted their money back. They were investing in us so that we would build large disruptive businesses and if we were indicating that we were willing to go slow, it went against their investing ideology. For venture capital firms, the returns mostly existed on the extreme—you either were an outsized success or a write-off. No one wanted to spend their time and effort on a middle-of-the-road company. Of course, there were other investors who understood that the frenzy of building and scaling up in the face of heavy capital raises needed to be paired with a period of sanity and the building of scalable systems. However, they also wanted to see a plan that they could get behind. Unfortunately, coming out of the boom in funding cycles, we only had high losses to show and couldn't completely figure out how to bring them down quickly without investing more in infrastructure and systems. It left us in a precarious place—of not knowing whether we could really keep investing in our new operations in the hope of becoming an investable business again in the future. Whatever we had learnt over the past year, it was clear that there were no strategic investors for businesses like ours, and if we needed capital in the future, we would have to turn again to private sources. That battle was still a while away though, as our immediate issues of learning how to build and operate large-scale physical infrastructure started becoming a worry, affecting the team's and my confidence and ability.

As to the murder at the beginning of the chapter—it turned out to be a drug deal gone wrong. While we never got the full details from the authorities, it seemed like the unfortunate reality of the parts of our society we don't see or acknowledge every day.

In 2015, we had rapidly scaled up our presence across cities and our consumer app had scaled up to serve almost 10,000 orders every day by the end of the year. We had done it largely in partnership with local stores and national chains. The ability of these stores to keep pace with us was worsening as we became larger and this affected both our consumers' experience and our financials. We had started investing in some dedicated warehousing infrastructure to steady the ship on consumer experience and had also raised a significant amount of capital through the year. However, we were entering 2016 with high losses, a slowing growth rate due to worsening consumer experience and a need to build out a lot more infrastructure in an environment where capital for loss-making companies had dried up.

2016

PIGEON POOP PROBLEMS

After we built our first warehouse outside of Gurgaon, we started realizing very quickly that a new world of learning awaited us. We had begun as a delivery company and had added the ability to operate small warehouses to that capability; most of the small warehouses we operated were in partnership with local shops. However, our newest endeavour meant we were now opening large warehouses by ourselves and trying to stock them by working directly with large brands like Nestlé and Amul. The first facility we signed up was in Gopalpur near Delhi-NCR, a warehouse that was around 30,000 square feet in area. This was a big change from the small 1,500-square-foot warehouses we were used to operating within the cities. Not only did these facilities have a much larger footprint, but they also had to be filled with rows upon rows of shelving racks so they could store more products. The Gopalpur warehouse had three floors and, compared to an average store which had storage space for a total of 15,000 items at any given time, it was able to store almost 6,00,000 items.

The first Grofers warehouse at Gopalpur near Delhi in 2016

A curious and very new problem we faced was that packaged products sent from this warehouse to customers had dried pigeon poop on them. Imagine ordering a plastic bucket for your shower and it comes covered in days-old pigeon poop. Not only did this make for terrible customer experience, it also caused a lot of issues with our warehouse employees as they did not like cleaning pigeon poop as a part of their everyday job.

The reason this was a new issue was that we had never operated such a large warehouse before and had not considered that when you have warehouses with high ceilings and large open doors for movement of goods and ventilation, pigeons fly in. A lot of products that were kept on the upper shelves on the third floor were right under the spots where the pigeons perched—and when the pigeons had to go, they had to go.

Another issue was that we usually kept slower-selling non-food items on the top shelves as they were ordered the least by customers. This reduced the effort our warehouse employees had to make to grab them. However, these items also had a higher commission for us and therefore selling them well was necessary. Complaints about these items were not a good thing for us as a business. Asking our workers to keep cleaning the poop wasn't feasible, when you consider we are talking about thousands of pigeons in a large warehouse with thousands of products.

This became enough of an issue for us to try and find experts to solve it. Of course, like with a lot of things in India, we have 'desi nuskhas' or hacks that are often implemented to solve problems like these (and which are ineffective, more often than not). One of the most bizarre hacks I saw implemented was at a warehouse that adopted a bunch of stray cats and kept them in the facility to control the problem of mice. It was a great solution till the cats started multiplying in scary numbers and attacking the milk packets.

In order to solve the ongoing pigeon problem, we tried hanging shiny compact discs and mirrors, both of which were grossly ineffective. The next bright idea from someone was to play loud music in the warehouse to scare away the birds. I think it was a ploy to have music played in the workplace all day, but I have never been able to prove it. The music experiment was stopped when a fight broke out among the warehouse employees from two different communities over whose choice of music would be played all day long. The list of experiments to solve the problem of the pooping pigeons continued for quite a while with no effective solution.

After a few months, the problem started to disappear on its own. What happened was simple—the overall platform started growing again and we started getting more and more orders for non-food items. This meant more of our workers were moving around on the top floors, which, in turn, meant the pigeons' peace was disturbed and they no longer wanted to sit inside the warehouse for too long. Over time, the problem disappeared almost entirely.

This has now become a common saying in our organization: 'Are we trying to solve a pigeon poop problem?' Very often we come across problems where we don't identify the root cause of the issue and spend a lot of time and energy trying to solve the thing that is bothering us—those are the real enemies of progress and, therefore, we call them 'pigeon poop problems'. Sometimes there are problems that don't have obvious solutions and the answer is not to address the problem itself but to do something entirely different or to live with it till the system evolves and the problem does not need our time or effort in the short term to be solved. In this case, the solution to the problem was to increase the number of orders, and the problem solved itself.

If we had taken a structured approach to solve the underlying issue of delivering on our promise to customers and focused on growth then we would not have let such a problem divert our attention. Till that time, our organization had found success by being reactive and nimble—with the mindset of doing whatever it took to get things done. These problems showed us that perhaps focusing on creating systems and processes and making structured progress was more essential than being jumpy and erratic. In short, it was time for us to adapt our way of working.

While across the world there are many examples of organizations and teams trying to solve pigeon poop problems, the prevalence of these problems in a developing ecosystem like India is quite high. Operating a business with on-ground touchpoints has complexities that are not existent for similar businesses in other countries. This is also part of the reason there is an opportunity to create iconic businesses in the country while it is still developing. Organizations have to keep their long-term objectives front and centre, and start overlooking daily problems that have no solution but can keep them bogged down endlessly.

If we were already a developed country, with consistency and strong implementation of design across the board, we would have a lot more competitive intensity in the country. A lot of things that are taken for granted in developed countries—for instance, consistency in infrastructure, sidewalks and dedicated parking—are chaotic in India, at best. I was dumbfounded when I found that Gurgaon has multiple kinds of pavements, sidewalks and drainage designs depending on which developer worked on which part of the city.[1] One of the biggest challenges to the development of a lot of our cities is going to be around bringing order and consistency to this chaotic development of infrastructure. More on that later.

Since the overall environment is chaotic and evolving at a rapid pace, founders and people working in early-stage companies, especially those with massive physical touchpoints, can spend their days and months solving problems that don't need to be solved. The detrimental effect of the presence of a large number of insurmountable operational issues is that you can end up losing sight of something that is more important and likely more valuable for the future of the organization. While we were dealing with pigeon poop, for instance, there was another story playing out in the same facility that would have a much larger impact on our future as a company.

From December 2013, at Grofers, our focus on technology was on building apps and products that either our consumers would use, or our delivery partners, local shop owners and merchants would find useful. The business was relatively simple since the inventory of products that we sold was fairly limited and most of the tracking work was done outside of our systems by the merchants and shops. However, as we started concentrating this inventory in large facilities outside the cities, in warehouses that we operated, we were suddenly accountable and responsible for tracking it. Even if the inventory belonged to brands or merchants, it was still housed in our facility and that meant we needed to know what all was there and how much of it—we needed to track it and share that tracking information with our partners. The easiest and fastest way to build this capability seemed to be to pick up a solution from the market—like a point of sale (PoS) and an inventory management solution—which typically came as a suite of services within a warehouse management system (WMS).

We were quickly able to find a couple of worthy providers who had everything we needed, and started the work of deploying one of the systems in the facility. The product was robust, had a lot of the features that we wanted and, to the delight of the finance team, integrated well with the tools that they needed to ensure our financial reporting happened in a structured manner.

The only problem was it didn't fit in with the way we wanted to operate the warehouses. What we had learnt over the previous three years of working with local partners and stores was that the only efficient way to operate was to move inventory quickly through our systems, make sure we tracked everything and, at the same time, rely more on our expertise in working with app-based systems, dynamic assignment and real-time tracking. The world in 2016 was already a place where smartphone penetration was increasing rapidly.[2] However, the software that we installed at our warehouses had not yet incorporated this revolution in the change of interface of how we were connected to the world.

As we were to discover soon enough, almost all the technology products that were built to support businesses were not created for the Indian ecosystem. Right from Enterprise Resource Planning

(ERP) to PoS management to location mapping software, almost everything had been built for the more developed markets where the solutions would find more takers. Sometimes they were repurposed for India but at the core they were not custom-built for the Indian ecosystem. This was of course understandable—why would companies spend millions on building software for a market where only a few players would use it? Not to mention, most service providers also complained that Indian companies were not good paymasters and negotiated too much, especially with smaller domestic players. As a result of this, even today, for simple technology answers like warehouse management solutions or financial management, we have to adopt global answers that are archaic, clunky and for which we don't actually have a large workforce that can be trained on them.

The PoS and WMS required chunky desktops and scanners to record any activity throughout the facility. Not only did they eat up space but also hampered the mobility of our warehouse workers, who could move around more efficiently based on real-time information, especially if that information was coming on their phones. Most of the warehouse workers in our facilities were young college graduates with only a rudimentary knowledge of computers. They were, however, mobile natives who could fix issues with mobile phones if they came up, but would be lost if the desktop malfunctioned.[3] They were used to operating touchscreen smartphones every day and understood how to navigate those well. We didn't have the time or resources to train hundreds of workers on how to use desktops—we wanted to leverage technology that they were already familiar with, which was mobile phones.

Even basic processes like updating information in our systems were slower as the existing software operated off local servers that took time to sync with master databases and provide us with an accurate view of what was going on. Coming from a world where we knew the position of every one of our delivery partners every thirty seconds, even when we had implemented rudimentary technology solutions for our last-mile work, the existing market solutions for tracking inventory and productivity seemed rather archaic.

Sticking with the external tools we had licensed would have meant being forced to adopt most of the known and existing warehousing practices, and accept that things would move at a certain speed and our visibility into the operations would also have a certain lag. Not to mention we would not be able to execute dynamic changes in real-time in the system based on what was happening. We would also have to invest more in training our workforce which was a big ask for a two-year-old unprofitable company.

Moving away from it was scary. It was a massive endeavour to build out such a complicated piece of software. The biggest fear was that we would be susceptible to inaccurate financial reporting during the period when we were using different tools for operational and financial reporting. An additional consideration was that we would be building this tool only for our operations and it would be expensive. There was no guarantee that the benefits would outweigh the cost of such large-scale development. Most of the time these tools were built by software companies that sold their solution to a number of organizations and therefore it made sense for them to invest in it. This investment would only make sense for us, if we became a really large company—having our own software would give us efficiency benefits.

However, at the time, this was a problem worth looking at, without necessarily worrying about how big we would get. We knew that having a tool that we had built in-house would give us more control in the future and that solving the problems that were caused by the inefficiency of existing third-party tools was not worth our while. We didn't want to try to tweak the existing system to be slightly better—we wanted to do something that would be remarkably better.

From our experiences, we had also learnt that we would have to invent whatever was needed. A few months before we were at this juncture, one of our investors had introduced us to accomplished folks from America who had built the supply chain for Amazon. They were there to look at the kind of problems we were dealing with, and figure out how we could benefit from their experience. After a day of going through our operations and facilities, both the parties arrived at the same conclusion. The challenges we were looking to solve were very different from the ones that Amazon had solved. The kind of problems that their Amazon experience could solve for us would come a lot later and would result in considerable expense. For now, we had to find a way to scale up without spending a lot of capital while overcoming the hurdles that our environment presented. In case you are wondering, the consultants had no idea how to solve the problem of transporting a truck full of eggs from a warehouse to the city if the road in between was completely dug up and broken.

Knowing that we needed to figure things out on our own, and knowing that we would have to build the technology for it ourselves, we told our technology team to get to work on creating our in-house warehouse management tool which we would start deploying in phases. The drop-offs that we would experience, both in terms of lack of essential features and risk of bad financial reporting—we could chalk up as pigeon poop problems; they would get solved on their own over time as the system got better. The crucial thing was that if we succeeded, we would be in a position to provide an accurate view of inventory to our customers and sellers at a fraction of the cost and that would be a game-changer. If we just stuck with the status quo and tried to solve incremental problems that third-party tools created for us, we would never be in a position to impact both customer experience and cost in a significant manner.

Also, in our thought process (on which there was widespread consensus within the organization), not having an in-house tool would be disadvantageous to us over the long term because we would be denying ourselves flexibility. We did not have a clue what that long term would look like, but had to take the short-term pain in our stride so we could be ready to build our operations in an environment that was predictably unpredictable. And there was pain.

We were able to get some basic features for operations out within a couple of months so we could start transitioning to our in-house tool, but the transition was painful and took long hours. In addition, when the software providers got to know we were working on an in-house tool, we became a low-priority account. As such, whenever we needed help or issues came up, it took a lot of effort to get them to respond. However, nothing compared to the pain we faced when, at the end of the year, we needed some data that our auditors had requested and it was not in our systems but with the WMS service provider.

They asked us for money to give us our own data, which, after a lot of negotiation, we agreed to do—as long as we had to pay only for the time they spent to get and give us the data. When we received the data, we realized the files were corrupted due to an error and the data was unusable. It took us six months of manually scouring through our facilities and collecting information to get our auditors the required data. And the pain wasn't about to end there. The system we were building was so large and complicated that it would be almost another year before we could start building the financial recording side to bring some semblance of normality and ease to our financial reporting structure.

Over the years, that one decision—to control our technology so we would have the freedom to build our operations and our infrastructure in any way we liked—proved to make the difference between life and death for our organization on multiple occasions. In the beginning, there was pain and there were trade-offs, but the effort was well worth it. Eventually, we gained efficiency at a faster pace, we could experiment a lot more and, when the time came to open up warehouses inside the cities again, we could just modify the system slightly to get up and running in no time. Not only that, when things changed rapidly around us, like with the introduction of GST and different regulations or innovations in our own operations, we adapted rapidly. The team that runs this system is still one of the largest teams within Blinkit, and it continues to innovate and build out the entire system—which has also grown now to include predictive systems, and is the nerve centre of operations and goods transfer across the entire country.

As I write this, this is the system that records, tracks, decides and executes the movement of 30 million products within our supply chain every day, generating over 650 million data points for us to analyse and act upon daily. Yes, it came at the cost of two years of pain in operations, in finance and even with our investors sometimes, who were getting antsy that we appeared to be building answers for the long-term instead of delivering high impact here and now. However, it was one of the best examples of overcoming a pigeon poop problem by focusing on what truly made a difference.

Focusing on what is needed for the long term becomes difficult to visualize when the problems we are facing become unrelatable. For instance, businesses in India eventually end up dealing with different political or local elements, sometimes even thugs. In city after city and neighbourhood after neighbourhood, the developmental dreams of a nation come head-to-head with the reality of a deep class divide. It is going to be a monumental task to pull enough people out of poverty and desperation and eliminate situations where legitimate businesses can be held to ransom by untoward elements, whether via pressure tactics on labour or harassment over operations. I remember getting a call from the head of Grofers in Mumbai saying that someone who was 'influential' in a particular area wanted exclusivity on running our local warehouse. Failure to work with them would mean our operations in the city would get disrupted. We refused. A few days after that there was a strike that originated in one part of Mumbai and quickly spread to almost the entire city. In another case, we were perplexed when the Department of Agriculture refused our application to store mosquito repellent (Good Knight or Mortein) at our facility, which they classified as a pesticide. We had invested almost ₹2 crores in the facility and waited around for a month to find out why we were being made to wait and how we could get the necessary permissions.

The wonderful thing about building a business that spanned technology and operations in India was the opportunity to witness the multiple touchpoints where it connected to the broader social fabric. However, these too were pigeon poop problems. We had to figure out a way to navigate them but we learnt over the years that these were not problems for which we needed to find solutions or spend our best resources. If we continued with our vision of building better consumer experiences then, eventually, we would see these problems disappear—simply because we could continue operating without solving them.

The way to spot these kinds of problems is to simply ask if solving them is something that will be a differentiator that customers will be able to point out and appreciate, or if it will change the cost or revenue structure of the company meaningfully. If it doesn't fit into either of these buckets, chances are it is a problem not worth devoting organizational energy to. These are irritants for sure, but scale, a larger brand, or even a larger team can make these go away. You can also choose to steer clear of these problem areas and know that you can always get back to serving these customers at a later date if it is an obstruction. I wish someone had told me this when we were dealing with these issues—it would have saved hours of my productive life, not to mention the stress I had to carry around thinking about the what-ifs. In the end, these problems are never fatal.

Early on in our journey, I encountered a deep point of frustration for me—why couldn't we just get on with the work we wanted or needed to do, without having to deal with the social mess around us? Through the last twelve years of this journey, I have witnessed various founders fall prey to these frustrations and become bitter or vindictive—they start believing that the system is out to get them, so they become more amiable to bending the rules or not caring about taking undue advantage where they can. Inevitably, the reality is that if founders or those in positions of power start to look down or take away from those without power, they will lose the trust of their own teams. It is an extremely delayed but powerful feedback loop.

I realized that my ability to deal with tough operational and on-ground problems had been shaped by the challenges of building in a developing country. At the same time, our teams' ability to overcome problems for the long term, influence their outcomes, and show resilience enabled them to uphold the rules—even when it would have been easier to bend them. These would be the differentiating factors for our organization. Just like the problems of pigeons in warehousing, a lot of the things we wanted to execute faced challenges that ranged from gravely serious to comedically random. It was up to us to choose to uphold a certain set of values and beliefs irrespective of how the world reacted or wanted us to react.

In the summer of 2014, when we were still a small company operating only a single station, I had to go one day to the offices of a large national retailer to pitch our services. I wanted to make sure I was dressed appropriately for the offices of such a large company as I didn't want to be hassled at the entrance. Even though I used to travel almost everywhere on a motorcycle in those days to avoid parking issues and would wear casuals with comfortable shoes, that day I decided to wear nice leather shoes to look more formal. As I got out of the meeting, I got a call from SK, who was back at the station, that all our delivery personnel had gone on strike. The reason for this was fairly benign: They did not like the behaviour of a new station manager whom we had hired to help us with the operations. The previous day, the station manager had made a new policy that delivery partners who wanted to deposit their cash with him had to come inside the station one by one. It was peak summer and people had to stand outside for some time to deposit their cash and go on to their next delivery. The manager was just doing his job. He had set up the new policy as there had been an attempt to commit fraud with many partners coming into the store simultaneously and handing over cash at once, creating confusion as to who had deposited what. They all claimed that they had deposited the full amount and someone else was short. It was clear that this was a synchronized activity and the station manager had taken action. He was familiar with such practices as he had spent a long time doing deliveries for other e-commerce companies himself and this was his first desk job.

A number of people among our delivery partners did not like this policy and proceeded to try and beat up the manager in the evening when he went to fetch his bike to go home. Somehow, the manager escaped with a few bruises and came in the next morning and reported what had happened. We had to take action and subsequently mandated that partners would have to sit outside the office as this behaviour was unjustified. This, in turn, had led to all of them refusing to work. While there were a few who wanted to work, most fell in line with the noisiest leaders of the group. We felt that we had to back the right thing to do and if that led to a strike then so be it.

Since we already had a number of deliveries pending that day, the station manager, SK and I decided that we would at least start doing the deliveries and somehow handle the assignments and the rest of the processes on the road. We also had a couple of folks who had left us, whom we called and offered to pay higher wages for them to help us out. We got a few people coming in and working that day, and slowly covered some of the backlog. A number of merchants showed understanding, recognizing that we were facing mutiny, and were patient, even telling their customers the deliveries would take a few hours. As I went about delivering one package after another, my leather shoes started scraping the skin off my ankle. These were not shoes meant for walking around for long periods of time and the sweat in the summer heat and the unexpected walking made it a whole lot worse. At some point, I had to go home and change into Hawaii chappals as my ankle was so bruised that it wasn't possible to wear any closed shoes. The pain, the sweat, the heat and the frustration of the situation were overwhelming, and I seriously questioned whether this was what I wanted my life to be. My optimism about the business and the opportunity, even my ambition—nothing mattered in that moment when the leather scraped against raw skin. All I wanted at the time was for the pain to stop—and there was nothing I could do using my intellect or experience. It was a simple choice between getting through whatever the pain of the day was or giving up. I remember that it was one of the toughest days to get through. The chaos in the middle of the heat and frustration were all little needles poking into me and sending the same message over and over again, that this was not a happy place for me to be. Looking back, it would have been stupid to give up over such a small thing. I am so glad that I held on that day. Yes, we still have strikes today and we often face a lot of issues related to discipline and the violation of our value system on the ground. Some of them are justified while others are not, and we have to deal with them accordingly. Today, there are issues that are irritants, but at the end of the day we need to have the resilience to survive the repercussions of sticking to our values, thought processes and vision for the long term.

During 2016, we were trying to transition to a business that relied on its own infrastructure rather than working with local shops and stores. Towards the middle of the year, we were under a lot of pressure to stem our losses—if we were going to invest in infrastructure, we had to shut down the most loss-making parts of the business. We subsequently stopped doing fast deliveries and only offered next-day deliveries to our customers. The result was that the business shrank in size and with an inferior delivery promise we struggled to achieve any meaningful growth through the year. Even though we were trying multiple things in our operations, the realization dawned that we would have to understand our customers a lot better if we were to invent a new way for them to buy their everyday needs from us.

2017

THE MIND OF A CUSTOMER

@albinder Need action from your team. This is not at all acceptable. Expecting a quick resolution on this issue.

—Tweet from a customer in 2018

One of the most interesting things about my Twitter (now X) mentions and those of pretty much any consumer-facing company executive in India is the sheer volume of aggrieved customers who tag the CEO, board members and, sometimes, even the Prime Minister of India to resolve a complaint that might be about an order worth ₹100. This 'I would like to see the manager' or 'Karen' phenomenon exists in other cultures as well, but it is significantly more pronounced in India than everywhere else. One of the reasons for this is that a lot of customers of e-commerce in India are those looking for deals and discounts, people who really value every penny.[1] Their sensitivity to problems like this is therefore higher than elsewhere. While this might be a part of the reason, there is a lot more to this phenomenon, as we witnessed over the last ten years of our journey.

A substantial chunk of these complainants are people looking to take undue advantage of the system. In a slightly odd representation of how systems evolve, many of the emails from aggrieved customers that land up in my inbox are from people who write a lot of the jargon that is used within our call centres and customer support teams. After the first few times this happened, I realized that a large number of people in India have had experience working in call centres and customer support teams, and as such are familiar with the processes of escalation and the policies within these teams.[2] With a substantial part of the population having trained in the Business Process Outsourcing (BPO) sector, we have created an ecosystem where companies in India, especially those facing customers, have policies and execution at par with or better than those offered by companies in developed economies. Many Indians are hired as backend support for customers abroad, and when they become consumers at home, they expect the level of service that they were expected to deliver in their day (or night) jobs.[3] I feel this sets a higher bar for consumer internet companies in India, and therefore, from day one we have to expect that the level of service will be compared to what our customers have seen in companies abroad, either as employees, travellers, or as backend support. Outside of this expectation, consumer internet companies in India still have to deal with a high level of attempted fraud—there is a thriving e-commerce version of Jamtara (the town widely considered the epicentre of online fraud in India and made famous by the Netflix series of the same name).

There are enough instances of people using their knowledge of how customer support teams work and taking undue advantage of customer policies. For instance, they know that the cost of providing support is higher than just refunding the customer in case there is a complaint against an error. They purchase products and then use this knowledge to get refunded, claiming quality or non-delivery issues. Also, in less developed countries, word about loopholes in customer service policies travels fast, and there are many people looking to make a quick buck. If there is a weak policy, it will be exploited very quickly. In our early days, it really made us nervous whenever it seemed like something was working well in our business. Our first instinct used to be to check for some version of fraud or policy misuse. This also created another distraction that could mask real consumer behaviour taking place on the platform. The noise from customer dissatisfaction and high volume of attempted fraud threatened to drown out the real insights to be gained.

This wasn't something unique to India alone. In order to understand how we started figuring out which core customer needs we had to focus on, we have to look at the journey of the organization learning about different consumer behaviours.

In 2017, I was in China to learn how delivery companies like Alibaba, JD and Meituan managed exponential scale and growth. At one such meeting with executives from Meituan, the discussion went into controlling customer fraud in the Indian context. It seems that globally all platforms—from food delivery to e-commerce—have a focus area around controlling fraudulent behaviour, whether relatively benign (abusive behaviour just to get a win) or serious (financial fraud on the platforms).[4] Till that time, it was my perception that due to lax enforcement and fewer worries of consequences in India, such activities would be much bigger in this country than elsewhere.

I was especially expecting China to not have this problem at a major level—since it is a tightly policed country with heavy-handed enforcement for even minor transgressions. To my surprise, the Meituan executives were very familiar with my problems of fraud. They proceeded to talk about their own fraud detection algorithms, the scale and extent of attempted fraud on their platform—by merchants, by customers, and even by their own customer service teams. The sheer numbers and scale were mind-boggling to me. When they told me about the size of the team that was perpetually working only on finding new kinds of fraudulent activity and curbing it on the platform, I was even more aghast.

After I had picked my jaw off the floor, I asked the burning question—weren't the people committing fraud worried about the consequences? The Meituan executive was bemused by what he could have only thought of as my innocence and proceeded to tell me how people did not think that fraud committed against e-commerce platforms was a crime. In their minds, it was validation of their smartness, and they were only exploiting platform loopholes instead of flouting legal terms and conditions. In case after case, where they had legally pursued customers accused of fraud—such as return fraud—they had found that the customer was almost always surprised that their actions, which were earning them money, were illegal and tantamount to theft. They also dealt with large-scale, coordinated fraud, but the perpetrators were way more careful about being tracked down or caught.

Now I can relate to this experience with fraud. One of my earliest such memories is from 2015, when our complaint rates on Grofers were just not reducing. The number of customers returning items at the doorstep or complaining about missing items in their orders was rising at an alarming rate. While we were occasionally making these mistakes at our end, in most of the cases there wasn't any evidence that we had made a mistake but, even so, we ended up issuing refunds. This was the time when we uncovered one of the largest scams that has been carried out in our systems.

One of our merchant partners, from whose stores orders were delivered, was placing orders himself, applying coupon codes meant for new users, getting the orders delivered to himself and giving a cut to the delivery partners to look the other way when he reported items missing and asked for a refund. In a matter of one week, there were a staggering two-hundred-and-fifty-plus orders placed by him, using different SIM cards. This was before the kind of organized fraud that makes our cellphones ring every five minutes now.

We decided to set an example for other customers and merchants and decided to report his violation of our agreement to the Cyber Crime department. Needless to say, they did not care at all. Despite our repeated pleas for action, the police's view was that this was a case of the company not being able to stop people from gaming the system. If a loophole existed, exploiting it—even if it was brazen fraud—might be illegal, but not something law enforcement would spend its resources on. The message was that they didn't think recouping money for companies was a priority for them. This was not a big enough matter for us to try to validate in a court of law, but it did hold a really big lesson: We could not expect to be treated like a victim under these circumstances.

We might have been a loss-making start-up, but we had to be ready to take the little things on the chin and watch our own way. In any scenario of perception, as either David or Goliath, we stood to be ignored. Neither were we the brash kind to try to pull strings to get things to move our way in the system, nor were we involved enough to understand the dynamics of the social machinery at work. Therefore, the only recourse for us was to figure things out on our own.

The outcome was the creation of a fraud detection team, of course, but also a change in how we thought about customer policies. This was the era in our journey that gave rise to constructs such as '₹100 off on every order (*only on orders above ₹1,000)'. These conditions were added so that the offers we provided were not abused outright. By making the consumers shop for more, we were making it harder for the abusive customers to use different phone numbers to avail the same offer. We started adding policies like these to our systems to explicitly restrict fraud.

As a result, our systems' design started leaning towards making customer policies that first and foremost took care of fraudulent behaviour on the platform. Almost everything was slowly moving towards a space where there was nothing useful left in our promotional offers and policies for good customers. Our fear of the bad actors was pushing our policies to a place where the platform was not able to delight the good customers and, as a result, we weren't able to use incentives to get the desired consumer behaviour. We were pushing our business more and more into a territory where we were not learning and evolving with customer behaviour because we were fixated only on controlling fraud. The side show had become the main piece.

Over time, we realized how we had gone too far in our efforts to control fraud and we could no longer make clean distinctions between different customer behaviours on the platform. We had to bring our focus back on the customer experience first, while building systems to stop fraud perpetually, on the side. To catch a few bad actors, we were making things difficult for a lot of customers. Going through this entire cycle had taught us that the majority of customers will just use the platform for its core functionality—the problem that it solves for them—and the ones looking to game the system are just noise that eventually reduces enough with scale to merge into the background. We realized that there were good customers out there, and in order to learn more about them we would need to be more experimental.

Since we were trying to systematically improve the quality of our business and also put more structured processes in place, we needed a better understanding of what our good customers were using the platform for. When we started looking at why the good customers were not engaging with us enough, we realized that the first job as a fast-growing start-up was to build trust on the platform. Customers in India, especially the ones online at the time, vacillated between fear, greed and uncertainty. The attitude towards e-commerce in 2014 was very different from the one we see today, even though there is still a large proportion of customers out there who do not buy online because they don't have trust—they fear they will not get what they want or that they will be taken for a ride. To overcome this fear, new companies resort to providing incentives to customers. This, in turn, also attracts fraudsters.

In a lot of ways, India's internet consumption in 2014 was closer in character to what was happening in America in the late '90s with internet browsers and online shopping.[5] People were discovering buying online for the first time and were wary of trying it out because they had never seen anything like it before. Compare this to the trust around e-commerce in the Western markets today, where customers know their money spent online is going to be safe.

Back in 2014 and 2015, this fear in Indian customers was even more pronounced as the market for e-commerce and customer exposure was much smaller. We were one of the first platforms to deliver groceries and that too in ninety minutes. For us, at the time, 30 per cent of the customers preferred to pay with cash on delivery and that number was significantly lower than what horizontal e-commerce companies like Amazon and Flipkart were seeing.

What was interesting in 2015 was that quick delivery (in ninety minutes then) was able to tap into something different for the customers where the time factor helped them to overcome their fear and lack of trust. Doing deliveries at speed seemed to uncover something in consumer behaviour that no one had seen before. The need for discounts and for convincing customers that the platform was trustworthy was lower—customers seemed to be willing to try out the 'everyday' use cases, or daily essentials, when delivery was speedier. The reduction in the number of cash transactions was proof that the need for trust is reduced when delivery is faster.

However, doing speedy deliveries was expensive. As soon as we moved away from 90-minute delivery to next-day delivery, we faced a sudden spurt in customer dissatisfaction, with fewer customers trusting the platform, more customers opting for cash on delivery and a lot of customers trying to game the system. The fact that customers got what they wanted relatively quickly, in ninety minutes rather than on the next day, seemed to generate less anxiety in an audience that had a high level of distrust in services in general. The moment we turned the service into one that delivered the next day, it immediately became irrelevant for a lot of customers—they dropped out due to the high level of anxiety of not knowing what would happen to their order if it was not delivered in the next few minutes. They didn't want to deal with that anxiety. This made us lose a lot of our early customers but left a lot of customers on the platform who had other motivations for ordering and who weren't necessarily anxious about not getting their orders. Some of these were also customers who were looking to target the loopholes in our policies to get a better deal.

At that point, our business was changing and struggling, and the only way we could get new customers to try out the service was through incentives and coupons, which caused our fraud rates to balloon, leading to even more losses. We were also keenly aware that some customers were choosing to come back and transact, even without these incentives, which meant the next-day delivery service was valuable to some customers. It also meant that there were other behaviours on the platform which we were yet to gauge and our interventions to control fraud made it a lot harder to understand a uniform customer behaviour.

One of the best examples of us influencing customer behaviour and reaching a wrong conclusion has been our journey with coupons. Coupons, much like in the physical world, are codes that customers can use on apps and websites to avail special, targeted discounts. Most of the time, coupons are limited to certain products and there are terms and conditions to control abuse. In the first few months of 2017, we experimented with an ill-conceived campaign where we tried to market discounts across products on Grofers and offered them via coupons. In the past, we had observed that whenever sellers had coupons offering special discounts on the platform our order numbers used to improve and we would have better retention of customers. As a result we thought this phenomenon was a clear indicator that this was what customers wanted—more coupons. We were wrong.

The campaign was a failure and there was a lot of conflict and debate internally on why it had failed. One thing was certain, though—customers were not after coupons; beyond a certain number, the coupons did not have any impact on the demand for our service. We were unsure as to why this was the case—we were now in a different model as a business from the one we had started with two years ago and that meant that many things were different. Instead of delivering on-demand, we were delivering after a day and, all of a sudden, it seemed that everything that was working for us in the on-demand model wasn't working anymore.

To understand the failure of our attempt to push more coupons to customers better, we looked at those who did use coupons on the platform and chose to transact with us continuously. By then our policies had become stringent enough to prevent abuse and every coupon user was looked upon with suspicion by the platform and by our people. The insight we came upon would power our thought process on how to find common behaviours across customer segments in a diverse income range country like India in the coming years.

A vast majority of the coupon users were, in fact, good customers, looking for value. It was important in their lives, so they were willing to overcome the platform hurdles, which included confusing on-boarding on the app, a bad payment gateway experience and delayed delivery. They put up with all of that because they did not have easy access to what they valued in their everyday lives—prices and variety. A home-maker living in the old part of Gurgaon had to travel at least 10 kilometres to access a supermarket. Their best option of finding prices that were similar to what sellers on our platform were able to offer was Sadar Market in Gurgaon, but that involved taking an auto or rickshaw, walking through the market on foot for a few hours and hauling all those products back. For home-makers with no support systems and a lack of available options of public transport, this was almost undoable.

These were the customers who were spending time on their phones, looking for an alternative way to access good-quality products for their families that would not be so punishing. The mobile phone revolution had connected consumers to e-commerce platforms, but the customers' changing expectations also suddenly opened up gaps on the supply side. When we talked to a few of these customers, it was fascinating—they wanted a platform like ours to give them value and access to products that would make their lives better and they were willing to live with our flaws, or to make trade-offs in customer experience, if we could give them what they wanted. This is what they were doing with coupons—reading the terms, picking items accordingly and, on occasion, even rewarding the platform with bigger orders because they thought the value we were providing was good enough.

When platforms are giving out coupons to users in Western markets, more often than not, they have a singular purpose to deliver monetary value of some kind and initiate a product trial. However, in our market, when you merge the lack of trust on new platforms and the attraction of discounts, the picture becomes a lot more complicated. Customers on our platform were looking for us to solve trust for them and then offer them value. When our sellers offered them value but they had to trust us to deliver the products a day later, a number of them simply chose to drop out. Those who continued to use the coupons were simply those who were already familiar with online buying, had trust and were therefore just using the coupons to access value that they otherwise could not.

When we analysed whether offering coupons helped to overcome the trust barrier, we realized coupons had a much lower impact on the behaviour of our female customers. Women shoppers in India were looking for the issue of trust to be solved first, before any incentives worked for them. So when they saw us offering coupons on the platform but not doing anything to solve trust, they didn't jump on board. Instead, the ones who were already using these coupons and already had trust just used more of them. In the battle between fear and greed, fear won for most of our female customers.

These women customers were not 'discount hunters' but everyday folk who wanted the platform to give them what they wanted—value for money and convenience. Weirdly enough, this fiasco with coupons made us realize our priorities—the platform needed to build trust and offer value in that order. What had started as an exercise to control fraud and seek more growth, had given us an insight into the way the customers chased value for money. The best version of this answer only came to us in 2020 when we started doing deliveries in ten minutes to overcome the trust barrier entirely.

In 2017, we had to shift our focus to figure out how the technology we were building could bring efficiency to the way goods reached customers so we could offer these customers value since that is what they were chasing, not just coupons. We also had to come up with something that made us earn our customers' trust every time. We chose the path of becoming a platform that aggregated only the best value-for-money products from different sellers and manufacturers. No gimmicks, no coupons, just a lowest-price guarantee from the seller shown to the customer upfront. Eliminating coupons not only signalled to customers that we were forthright in our proposition, but also made our job of tracking fraud a lot easier.

Over a two-week period, we went about overhauling our business so we could talk about value with all the manufacturers, brands, sellers and suppliers that we worked with. We got a lot of feedback on what it would take for manufacturers to supply products that would make customers believe they were truly getting value for their money every time they shopped on Grofers.

For instance, the manufacturers said that they would be able to sell products at lower prices per unit (per kg or per litre) if they could sell in large sizes (only packs of 3 kg, 5 kg, and so on). We started asking our customers if they would take the trade-off and they did. Instead of coupons, they were happy to buy more and save that way. They already understood why things bought in bulk were cheaper so they believed us when we offered this proposition on the app. When they used a coupon, they wouldn't know whether they would get the product for the same price the next time they wanted it. They felt that using a coupon was a one-time offer so they didn't invest in crossing the trust barrier. They would continue to be cynical the next time they transacted with the platform, even if their previous experience had had no issues. As the transition to prioritize value started becoming more successful, manufacturers and sellers changed what they sold on the platform so as to deliver more value to customers—and the customers loved it.

Looking back, we started to notice a pattern in how customers responded to coupons and what that said about how Indian consumers built habits. For a large set of customers, coupons or one-time deals were very quickly forgotten. They just assumed that if an unknown platform was offering coupons then they must have already built in the cost of the offer. If the coupon was, however, of a known branded product and if that was the best deal they had seen for the product, then the customer felt confident about using it and wanted it repeatedly. For platforms like ours, building trust via coupons on known brands requires offering them consistently over a very long period of time—something that eventually becomes financially untenable for the seller and the platform. So, while these consumers were quick to respond to coupons, they were also unlikely to register the value or remember the transaction. They were confident online buyers who just took advantage of whatever deal was out there. Then there was another set of customers who wanted something different from us. They wanted the feeling that they were getting the best value from us every day and that feeling of getting value had to be reflected across every one of their touchpoints with us. These two sets of customers also represented a gender skew—the first category was overwhelmingly made up of men and the second overwhelmingly of women.

Once we had determined that we wanted to be in the business of delivering value to women customers, we were on a roll again, and month after month we could see that our focus on delivering value was getting picked up by customers. It was also leading us to become a better business as our sales and commissions started increasing with the volumes on the platform going up. Over the next two years, up until COVID-19 hit, we were only focused on this proposition—how to make the supply side more efficient so that customers got the best possible value, and for us to deliver this value again and again to enhance trust. This wouldn't happen by throwing out blind subsidies but by bringing real innovation to the movement of products, technology, inventory management and smart partnerships that were good for business and provided value for customers. Our research into the value segment also made us realize that women customers were not being aptly served by Indian e-commerce. A startling insight that stuck with me was that in most socio-economic segments, outside of the really rich in India, even though women were shopping on e-commerce platforms, they still had to ask their husbands to make the payments. This was reflected in the fact that orders with names of women customers typically had payment methods with men's names. As we went about creating value for these customers, our systems also had to start solving their other problems, like easy access, delivering at times which suited them and offering products that they had trouble finding offline. We started referring to these customers as 'she' and 'her' and made delivering value to her our mission statement. Fun fact: a large number of our customers during those times would shop on our app after 10 p.m., once the entire family had retired and the day's work was done.

To this day, even after becoming a platform that delivers in ten minutes, we have held on to this ethos of delivering value. If we are able to extract ₹1 of efficiency in the supply chain, we will pass almost all of it to the customers. This number became 100 per cent after we became profitable overall and will continue at 100 per cent forever. We believe passing on efficiency gains to customers saved us once and it is the right thing to do—so we will always stay at it, consistently. It is common retailing knowledge that the customer you have is more precious than the customer you want. So if we want to keep the customers we have, we have to keep providing them with more and more value. That value can be in different forms—lower prices of products is just one of them. Faster deliveries is another. Over the years, we have tried to add many dimensions to this value. Think for a second about a product like Apple's iPhone. Apple has to come out with a lot of innovative features just to be able to charge the same price for the phone next year. Now, imagine if they stopped doing this value addition. Would the customers pay the same price for the same phone next year? Likely, they won't.

As early-stage businesses look at their customers and try to market to them, they are often not aware of the social factors affecting the adoption of their products. We had tried a number of ways to grow our business, only to realize that what our customers needed from us lay elsewhere on the spectrum. We also had to find the customer who needed our service the most and align our service to their needs to a greater degree. The solution towards value and access was an insight that drove our business out of the funk it had found itself in when the fast-delivery market imploded in 2016. We had reached this insight by pursuing the needs of the customers who needed us the most. It was, however, hard to overcome the trust barrier with long delivery times in this business. This was to be an important insight later on. The trust barrier for customers is much lower in 10-minute delivery than in next-day delivery but, sooner or later, everyone is going to overcome the trust barrier as the market evolves and more customers become familiar with buying online. When that happens, the proposition of value and efficiency will help the platforms stand out—with their ability to deliver products with good execution, and with the customers trusting that they will receive their orders.

Grofers found a new lease of life in 2017 by focusing squarely on customer needs and building a very focused proposition around delivering value to customers in the form of speciality products and better offers from sellers and brands. We started growing rapidly and, in lockstep with this growth, had to start investing in even more infrastructure and technology as our scale almost tripled that year alone. We were, however, also finally starting to run out of the capital we had raised almost two years ago and were entering the new year feeling a lot more confident but also more anxious about raising capital again.

2018

WORKING HARD FOR ESOPS

In the first real office space that we rented for Grofers in Sector 18, Gurgaon, there was a peculiar Gurgaon-special scene in 2014. The office was located behind the WAPCOS office in the Udyog Vihar area in a rather old building, which used to be a godown for storing paint thinners. On the first floor, above the smell of the paint thinners, we had a bunch of disjointed offices where our different teams conducted business. While the office had the real character and ethos of a company without capital, yet sometimes it felt we had overdone it on the cheapness index, especially because we learnt later that having an office above highly flammable products like paint thinners was not the brightest of ideas.

Under the window of my office on the first floor was a huge water tank that supplied water to the building. Next to the water tank, in an area that could not be reached unless you crawled under the tank or climbed over the wall next door, used to live a family of pigs. On any given day, there used to be about six or seven of them and they got really loud. The piglets would be fighting for the most part and, as I was to learn later, the adults spent a lot of time mating. Since I had chosen an office with a window that opened on this side, the noise pretty much only bothered me and there was no solution. This was no professionally managed office building where you could call someone to take care of the noise. I tried, uselessly, to shout at them to get them to disperse, but could never bring myself to throw stones at them, like the building's security guard sometimes did.

The noise of the pigs having a good time became the soundtrack of my office. The room didn't have air conditioning, so the window had to be kept open on most days. This was the room in which I conducted interviews and met with potential investors and merchants. When I needed peace and quiet I would go to the room where our developers used to sit. Not to perpetuate the stereotype, but there was a trade-off for sitting with the developers—it required me to urge them to wash their socks. That was a battle I never won.

For a few months, the soundtrack of squealing pigs and their daily lives was a part of my work routine. I remember running to the other side of the building to take an important call with an investor because I didn't want to lose my train of thought if the pigs started fighting. I used to wonder how strange it would sound to people on the other end of the line if I told them the reason for putting them on hold while I moved to the other side of the office. I was starting to develop a strange sense of familiarity with some of the pigs, as if they were house pets.

In December 2014, I had a potential investor visit the office early in the morning. Since only my room was open and the pigs had decided to have a noisy morning, we decided to walk to the empty plot next door and sit at a tea stall there to enjoy a winter morning cup of tea and talk shop.

As we sat there, two guys arrived on a scooter. They headed straight for the water tank and shot a few stones under it without hesitation. There was commotion in the pig mosh-pit and the creatures started running around, resulting in a little one ending up in the empty plot. One of the men on the scooter picked up a big piece of rock and proceeded to smash it on the head of the little pig. He missed connecting properly the first few times the pig was running, but eventually succeeded. The little convulsing animal was then picked up, put on the floor of the scooter, after which the driver proceeded to put his feet on it to stop it from convulsing, and then drove away.

That was the day I found out these were domesticated pigs. They were not there by accident of birth—someone had claimed them as their property and that someone was a meat shop in the village of Sirhaul in Gurgaon.

The state of the meat industry and the general quality and hygiene control in our food chain are not why I am telling this story. To me the incident demonstrated the way our mindsets work as a society and the implications it has on business.

Around the same time that I was building a relationship with the pigs downstairs, we were also looking to hire and build up our technology team. We had onboarded the first few developers that we were able to hire with our limited budget, but desperately needed to add smart young folks to the team. One of the early hires, Ankur Saxena, was helping me recruit people, both from within our network and from campuses. We were travelling to small Tier-2 and Tier-3 colleges to recruit people who had a passion for coding and who were contributors to either the open source community or were active on forums that discussed issues around programming. We were also hungry for underappreciated talent that did not command the kind of salaries that graduates from Tier-1 colleges like the IITs were demanding.

We found one such hire from Jaipur. Ankur, who had a good sense of the colleges there, had interviewed a few people online and had made an offer to a fresher who was looking to enter their last semester in college, which they would spend as an intern at a company. The person we zeroed in on was a very relatable young technologist for both Ankur and me, and reflected the technologist's ethos that we were familiar with. Young, docile, awkward, with facial hair that he would not groom (even into his late twenties), not physically active but highly gifted in computer science.

The last bit was the only part relevant for us, so we decided to stretch our fairly limited budget at the time to hire the twenty-year-old. We decided he would spend the semester working with us as an intern and then would join us as a full-time developer (assuming the company survived that long). Even though we did not make the best offer, our vision of building something cool, the passion that Ankur and I had for technology, and the promise of working in a small set-up with other geeks, swayed the decision in our favour. We were excited—we would get someone who was passionate about Python (the programming language at the heart of our technology systems) and fairly knowledgeable about it. We figured it would likely double our ability to develop our systems.

The day of his joining, our new intern showed up from Jaipur with his parents in a white Swift Dzire—the preferred ride at the time of the upper segment of the 'Indian middle class' (as the top 2 per cent of our country like to identify themselves). The family got down from the car to find pigs casually lounging by the building entrance. That scene was, by itself, enough to convince the parents that this wasn't the place where they wanted their son to be working. As a few of us who were hanging out by the tea stall watched from a distance, they got back in the car and left, never to be heard from again.

Even though, at the time, I was furious that our society was so shallow as to dismiss a book by its cover—when I really thought about it, it made sense.

I could almost picture my parents dropping me there at twenty-one and not accepting that this would be a place of work worthy of their son's education and their social standing. They would have asked me to come back to our hometown and try something else, which was not this—because we had the luxury to do so. To them, and to most of India, all work is not created equal. Generations of living with a caste system has made Indians naturally attuned to equating jobs with social stature. This experience also made me realize why the outsourcing sector had invested in glitzy campuses for relatively entry-level jobs. The spectacle had played a big part in making these roles socially acceptable. Back in 2014, working at a start-up was not a career choice that was accepted as the norm—we didn't have these glitzy campuses yet.

Over the years, this problem has started receding into the background because of two major factors. One factor is the increasing coverage of the success stories of start-ups and their founders, and the economic prosperity that has followed for both founders and employees of emerging companies.

The other factor has been the growing consciousness of entrepreneurship, through the multiple TV series about emerging companies raising capital from more experienced founders. Even before the success of these TV shows or other start-up stories, a lot of people had started gravitating towards start-ups. While a large proportion was drawn in because the work seemed to be exciting and different—a change driven by the Internet age and global exposure—there were still quite a few who joined this world because they saw how successful some of their peers were with respect to wealth creation.

In 2014, the attitude towards start-ups was still cautious, and as a result we not only struggled to hire fresh or inexperienced graduates, but also had trouble getting experienced professionals to join us. You would think that professionals in their mid- to late-career stages would have better information and a better understanding of ecosystems and be more open about joining an early-stage company. This was (and is still) not the case due to three reasons primarily. First, the prospect of working at a start-up versus working in an established organization like Facebook (now Meta) or Google was less prestigious. Established multinationals were considered better for long-term prospects by professionals—this included the lure of also relocating out of the country. Second, start-ups usually struggled to match the dollar-denominated salaries offered by established companies. Third, there was a lack of trust and understanding of ESOPs in the ecosystem in general.

ESOPs, or Employee Stock Option Plans, are an important tool used by emerging companies to attract talent. This concept was introduced in India initially by the outsourcing sector; companies like Infosys were pioneers in awarding stocks to their employees. If you look at more traditional business houses or the majority of listed companies in India, only the promoters or founders hold stock in the company. The rest of the employees are, by and large, only able to access the company's stocks in the public market. Stocks as a mode of compensation and alignment of incentives for employees were not utilized widely until the outsourcing boom and subsequently the start-up boom.

With the funding for start-ups increasing, a number of people who had followed traditional career trajectories suddenly found themselves looking at start-ups as a good way to progress financially given the prospects of increasing their wealth materially via ESOPs. As the mid- and late-stage capital raised by start-ups grew larger, they were also able to match salaries in entry level and mid-level roles with a number of other industries while still maintaining the mainstay of providing generous ESOPs as compensation above and beyond the salaries.[1] From 2007 to the early 2010s, start-ups gave out ESOPs generously to invite experienced professionals whose salaries they could not generally afford. The prospect of creating wealth by taking a risky bet on a newly founded company was one that appealed to experienced folks—the potential reward was so high that the risk did not seem to matter. Some of these early success stories, encouraged a number of people to think of start-ups as a good way to create wealth.

This is a little puzzling because the success rate of start-ups, especially in the technology space, is notoriously low. For every success story you hear today, there are probably a hundred failures that you never get to hear about. However, during the boom in funding, a lot of folks began to believe that every such start-up which had raised capital would succeed. This happens during most boom cycles. Over time, salary cuts almost disappeared from start-ups as funding rounds came earlier and in larger sizes.[2] You could argue that well-funded start-ups are now generally the paymasters in many industries and do tend to attract the best talent quickly.

As such, a number of folks found themselves joining start-ups with almost no risk assessment because the employers were offering them a competitive salary. The ESOPs only seemed like the cherry on top, a bet that could potentially pay off handsomely if things went well. As such, a lot of talent flowed to start-ups, whether or not they were established or successful, so it became about which startup was willing to use their capital to pay incoming talent higher salaries. Providing ESOPs as a substitute for higher salaries to experienced individuals used to lead to genuine conversations between employers and employees about the latter's reasons for joining a company. This phenomenon has largely disappeared, with the unfortunate side-effect that the role of ESOPs and discussions about them have also grown muted.

The fact was that probabilistically, start-ups were, and still remain, bad for creating wealth.[3] Very few companies make it and, among them, fewer create big enough outcomes for wealth. So, if you have one career to bet on in the next ten to fifteen years, success at start-up is a low-probability event. For folks who are not driven by a passion for working in a particular space, the risk-adjusted outcome of start-ups is lower than working in an established company.

Having said that, ESOPs are still among the most powerful tools we have on hand to re-shape the attitude towards work and opportunity in this country.

Let me illustrate with our experience.

For founders, a few years in their career often stand out—usually for the difficulties or seemingly endless challenges they faced. In hindsight, overcoming those obstacles does bring a somewhat perverse satisfaction. These challenging periods—whether caused by a lack of options or by having choices forced upon you—give you the freedom to experiment with almost anything and discover where you truly stand on a range of issues, from your moral compass to how much you are willing to sacrifice to keep going. As much as you may want this pain to end, something pushes you to keep going.

For Grofers, and particularly for me, 2018 was a year that felt like a decade. At the time, we were desperately trying to convince investors that the company, with the new next-day delivery model and its focus on everyday value for customers (especially targeting a middle-India female demographic), was back on track and worth investing in again. We needed capital to scale up our operations further; even in our mature cities, our operations were not at the point where the infrastructure we had put in place would start getting utilized enough to generate profits. We had successfully shifted business models to a next-day delivery service and, after a tough period in 2016, had started finding our feet in early 2017. We were getting the hang of warehousing, customer experience was improving and we were going sharper on the proposition of providing a differentiated assortment of products to customers who did not have a supermarket or value-shopping experience close to their homes. As a result, the business was growing and revenues were improving every month.

A number of things were working for us, except one. We were considered the poster child of excess from 2015 and there had been enough and more speculation (understandably) from existing investors about whether we were a worthwhile business to keep backing. However, it didn't make sense that the negative sentiment about our past fundraising and subsequent failures alone could convert the potential of the business in two years from one that had a massive future to one that didn't have any. Between November 2015 and January 2018, we had grown 600 per cent with the losses being lower in January 2018 than they were in 2015. We were growing and doing something unique even within the highly competitive segment. BigBasket was the market leader, with conglomerates and large e-commerce companies also stepping in—everyone from Reliance to Flipkart and Amazon had launched their e-commerce play in grocery at the time. Despite that, we were telling a compelling enough story in numbers. Except that it was hard to convince any investor that we had turned a corner and that they should take a chance on us. The hard work of the last couple of years and the resilience of the team didn't seem to matter to investors, and rightly so.

On their part, investors had new and exciting opportunities to back, which had not faced the kind of public criticism that we had. Why even bet on whether we would turn things around from a negative space when they could invest in other opportunities where their choices would not be publicly questioned? Other than the fact that there seemed to be hope in the numbers we were demonstrating, the only thing going for us was that there was still a decent amount of capital already invested in us and the overall grocery space seemed promising enough for the future of the business, especially given that we were approaching a decent scale at sales of almost ₹100 crore a month.

We had boldly rebuffed our investors a year ago when they wanted us to shut down and return the remaining capital in the business, and we felt we had done enough to deserve a chance to continue.

After a few months of back and forth with existing investors, we found a way forward. There would be capital available for us to keep going as long as we continued to demonstrate that the business was growing and becoming healthier. The capital came with a lot of strings attached. We were raising a total of $45 million but the money was coming in tranches of $10–15 million each once we met some targets. So every few months we would have to prove again that we were hitting the milestones to deserve the capital for the next few months. More important, though, the investors planned to cut the company's valuation by 50 per cent, which would give them a larger stake. The nature of this structure also meant that we couldn't really look for outside capital (not that anyone was lining up to invest in us at the time).

The first set of conditions was a nightmare for running a business but taught us a lot of discipline—we could not look beyond the next few months and had to be frugal with any cash we were spending. We had to accelerate our efficiency plans over everything else and be really thoughtful about where we were investing. The fact that we kept building our technology for warehousing through this period was one of the major achievements, and a rather brave call we took, and one that might have gone horribly wrong. Month after month, we kept chasing the milestones. Meanwhile, we continued to engage with new and old investors to get more capital for the business. Any small issue in the middle would cause sleepless nights because it could potentially result in us falling behind any of the milestones we were chasing.

We were still growing as an organization but had to take extreme calls on cost control so we could continue our day-to-day operations and build the infrastructure to cater to customers. In hindsight, it was a wild time as we were breaking ground on our largest warehouse in Delhi-NCR at the time, which was 2,00,000 square feet and, at the same time, had no idea whether two or three months down the line we would be able to secure more capital to keep the business going. Our office in Udyog Vihar in Gurgaon was over capacity, to the point where we had covered the parking area to create temporary meeting rooms and renovated the existing meeting rooms inside to create more seating space. Even the open spaces in the office were covered up to create more seating space. At one point, we were seating almost five hundred people in an office that was meant to accommodate two hundred. However, we didn't have the capital to get a new office. If we had any money, we were investing it in building our warehouses or investing in our last-mile network. In the middle of all this, we of course had many issues to deal with daily. With larger e-commerce players entering the space, we learnt one day that one of the leading FMCG companies was going to cut down advertising spends on our platform by half as their management mandate was to focus on the larger e-commerce platforms rather than on Grofers. Since they were the largest advertisers on our platform, our monthly revenue would take a big hit. It was also a decision that was hard to understand, as we were growing fast and were the second-largest platform after BigBasket. For a few sleepless nights it felt as if this development would be the final blow for the company, and we would see a similar exodus of multiple brands. We would fall behind on our milestones, and the company would be forced to shut operations. Thankfully, better sense prevailed and within a month the brand realized that reducing ad spends on Grofers was not a good idea.

This stressful period for the business continued almost all the way through the year. Between living from milestone to milestone and balancing between really short-term and long-term decisions, we were now valued at half of what we had been valued two years ago. This meant that for the founders—SK and me at the time—shareholding in the company was cut in half as all the remaining investors had anti-dilution rights. It is a fairly common practice in private investment markets for investors to have superior rights compared to founders. For example, if an investor owns 10 per cent of a company and values their stake at ₹10, the implied company valuation is ₹100. If the company's valuation subsequently drops to ₹50, the investors' stake is protected at Rs 10, which now represents 20 per cent of the company. In such a scenario, the founders end up giving up a larger portion of their equity.

However, it wasn't just the founders who were losing value on their holding. Any employee who had shares in the company worth ₹100, for instance, now saw the value of their ESOPs cut down by 50 per cent to ₹50 as well. This was difficult for people who had been working hard to keep the company going for the last two years, ignoring the general criticism outside, keeping their heads down and focusing on their job. Even when the pressure of meeting milestones every week and managing the business in an uncertain environment was at its highest, we were effectively telling these stakeholders that the shares they held in the company were suddenly worth only half of what they had believed. A lot of them had joined our mission over the last few years and it would create a decent dent in their confidence to learn this. SK and I took the decision that we would treat the ESOPs of the employees like we were treating the investors—they would not be diluted. We would issue additional ESOPs to employees to make sure that the value of their shares was not reduced.

Our read at the time was that the people putting their faith in the organization, and those who were still making an impact, were doing so because they felt they had a sense of ownership in the company. If that ownership fell materially, they might not feel the same way. Even for us founders, it was a hard call to continue going after such a big reduction in value, but it was nevertheless something that we felt was the right thing to do. Someone who had been there for only a couple of years would likely not feel the moral responsibility to continue working on the business if the potential financial upside went down significantly.

Additionally, while as much as a handful of our people at the time were committed to the cause, the vast majority still treated this as a job. They wanted the security and surety of a job first and foremost; the fruits of growth came later. Our white-collar ecosystem still has this invisible force that wants companies to operate like benevolent benefactors instead of the capitalist organizations that they are. People don't want to be made to feel like cogs in the machine, to only work on incentives or disincentives. This leads to a dichotomous organization in many cases—one that builds capitalistic systems, because that is how the organization is judged, but cannot apply these systems uniformly within the organization. We had already learnt that we needed to ensure that the organization's morale was not impacted by this event, and that the people who were just starting to believe that their ESOPs mattered were protected.

We had direct experience of this dichotomy for the first time in 2016 when Grofers pulled back campus offers days before people were set to join. While we deservedly got a lot of grief for it from parents, colleges and the social media intelligentsia, the lesson was fairly straightforward. We had to be more thoughtful about the motivations and incentives of those choosing to work with us. We could not assume that everyone accepted that working at a start-up was a high-risk, high-reward endeavour. This dichotomy between the volatility at early-stage start-ups and the expectation placed on them is a broad generalization, and we have overcome many hurdles and made significant progress in this regard over the years. However, we will need to reconcile with the fact that this dichotomy is going to exist till the success stories of enough people and start-ups wipe out the memories of generations who worked in more protected set-ups that reflected a more socialist approach in our country's business environment.

Employee ownership of company equity has been a powerful tool in breaking through this transition. It has an even greater role to play in developing talent and shaping the workplace in start-ups than it does in other companies. It has shown people that their choices outside established norms can generate successful and life-changing outcomes. It instils a sense of purpose in individuals and lets them have a real share of the impact of the organization's work. Even though the probability of success of an organization might be low, it creates the kind of ambition for success needed to change peoples' attitude towards risk and reward.

The opportunity of wealth creation that growing companies can provide is a concept that is hard to understand and grasp.

Even now, there are plenty of people who have made life-changing money by working at start-ups. Millionaires from Flipkart, Zomato and even Blinkit are examples of people who took the road less travelled and ended up earning far more money during the same period than executives in traditional corporate roles could have imagined. In fact, over the last few years, ESOPs are emerging as a way for start-ups across the country to build the kind of legitimacy that IT companies built between 2000 and 2005 with their swanky offices and international vibes. For the first time in the Indian start-up ecosystem, there are enough and more cases of folks who can point to the amount of money they were able to earn from their ESOPs as proof that working at a start-up is worth it.[4] This is the counterbalance needed to move things to a more capitalistic and, in my view, a more meritocratic way. The mutual respect between employees and employers will deepen if the good of the company is at the centre of both their end objectives. Traditional businesses in India almost never offered their employees the option of owning a share of the company. Start-ups (starting with the IT majors) have done that over the last couple of decades and they have the potential to create a new way of working that will likely create a talent rush for white-collar work at new-age companies, triggering a virtuous cycle that compounds positively. The educated workforce can own a share of the business and, with the potential financial freedom that doing so offers, perhaps they can be the next generation of founders that will have an even larger impact on the ecosystem by creating further opportunities for others.

Even as the popularity of entrepreneurship has generated enough and more interest in new-age companies, brands and the overall ecosystem of backing early-stage companies, many employees—and the other decision-makers in the tribe, their families—remain sceptical and, to some extent, ignorant of how

ESOPs work. It is almost imperative that start-up founders start using ESOPs in a much bigger way to drive ownership so that we can collectively celebrate the outcomes that people have benefited from. Doing so will go a long way in changing peoples' attitudes about the nature of work. Just like the entry-level workforce has trust issues that also emanate from some version of a socialist mindset about the nature of work, the white-collar workforce has not completely adapted to a more capitalistic set-up. The fact is that the success stories created by using ESOPs more widely to drive ownership will be the strongest proof for broader society to start accepting employment at big companies and start-ups as equivalent. The entire investing ecosystem, both private and public, also has to get behind this process of giving ESOPs the central place in value creation that they deserve. Companies are built and value for shareholders is created by the quality and motivation of the entire team, not just that of the founders. Every time public investors, boards or even private ones nickel-and-dime employees on ESOPs, they are inadvertently pushing us back into a promoter-driven era and away from a vibrant ecosystem of meritocracy and collective motivation.

When Grofers (renamed Blinkit by then) was later acquired by Zomato, our ESOP holders had to wait for over six months before they could sell their shares. By that time, the price of Zomato's stock had dropped significantly from the time when we had started working on the deal. While a number of people held on for some more time and sold their shares when the stock price soared, even those who sold their shares at the relatively low point in the stock price journey chimed in with messages of gratitude and love. For a number of them, it was life-changing money that would allow them to pursue their calling, send their children towards a better educational future or buy a house. A few of them ended up starting their own businesses. A number of people who benefited were also there with us in 2018 when we had made the fortuitous decision to not let the value of the company affect the value of the ESOPs. While we had done it with the goal of fairness and self-preservation in mind, what I learnt over time is that preserving the sanctity of the value of ESOPs for a company like ours was a strong signal of our culture and values. We were instrumental in legitimizing for our employees the idea that they were not just working for a salary but owned a share of the business and that share was taken seriously. The biggest disservice start-up founders have done in the country is neglecting the distribution of ESOPs and being nonchalant about treating them fairly. The ESOP holders' equity needs to be treated better than the equity of the shareholders and founders. In reality, it is usually treated the worst. The trend of ambitious and smart employees who choose to spend their time in organizations that give them a shot at owning a part of the outcomes of their efforts is only going up. This is going to forever change how employment and opportunity are viewed by a generation. We will disassociate more and more from the older ways of thinking about jobs in terms of security and stability, and the more ambitious will start weighing opportunity over everything else.

Over the last few years, being part of a public company, we have seen this feeling multiply as a greater number of employees have received more shares. As the value of the business has gone up, so has their net worth. What was popularized as a trend by IT companies to share wealth with their employees can now have a much bigger impact due to the number of start-ups and their prevalence across the ecosystem. I do hope that unlike the IT ecosystem, where only a handful of companies were able to scale and create wealth for their employees, the start-up ecosystem in India produces multiples of similar outcomes. The beneficiaries of these programmes are as diverse as the development vectors of India's progress. The early employees of Grofers were sons and daughters of small business owners or government officials. Most, if not all, had moved to large cities from small towns, much like SK, Rishi and I had, to seek forward momentum in life. A large part of our success is actually the result of the ownership, dedication and capability of these people. They took the important decisions about the business day in and day out that propelled an entire industry. I have been lucky to have many people around me over the years who I felt needed to own more and more of the company that they were building.

I believe ESOPs are probably the best way of making sure that enough benefit of the country's growth and development touches the lives of the folks who are doing the work of building new kinds of companies. We don't want to be mired in a plutocracy where only a few end up being the beneficiaries of the development of the country. When we look at businesses that are benefiting from growth, whether in infrastructure or other fields, we have to start asking the question: How many people are going to partake in these growth opportunities? Sometimes it is mind-boggling that ESOPs are taxed so highly when the people receiving them are responsible for building the companies. These people deserve to be treated like value creators, like founders themselves, and therefore should be paying the same taxes as those paid on capital gains. Rishi and Anish Shrivastava have been with me for over ten years now; Udit Gupta has been with Zomato for over twelve years. All of them are integral parts of these companies and are the reason the companies are where they are today. However, when they sell their shares, they have to pay a tax of 40 per cent versus someone like me who has to pay less than half of that today. This isn't fair and puts the institution of wealth creation by building organizations at risk.

ESOPs are also the largest tool we have to break up the notion of segregation at work. The journey of building something is humbling—you have to do whatever it takes to build the company. For three years, SK was the record holder in Grofers for the number of deliveries done, followed by me. It meant we had gone out and made these deliveries. A lot of the early employees, including those whose core role did not include making deliveries, stepped in because they felt like owners. Their focus was only on the company's progress, helping wherever needed. If we are to truly move forward as a society, then dignity of all types of labour has to be elevated and we have to leave behind the legacy that certain jobs are only meant for certain people. To demonstrate the depth of this segregation, even to this day, the toughest battle in every store and every warehouse is over the requirement of 'housekeeping' to perform every basic cleanliness chore. Not only will people not do anything outside of their primary activity, the majority thoroughly detests the idea of doing something as basic as wiping down a toilet seat. That is a task left for someone else. It is bias and segregation in plain sight and we are letting it happen—yet still hoping that the country will make progress. When we create business owners, people develop a sense of ownership that is unlike anything an employee will ever feel working for a wage. When society values ownership as a sign of social stature, everything else falls by the wayside. Owners will focus on building their company and making it a success as ownership itself becomes a status worth aspiring to.

As we entered 2019, the Grofers business was in a relatively better position. After a few faltering starts with next-day delivery, we had found our footing in operations and customer positioning by focusing on the value segment. After being on a milestone treadmill for a few months, we had proven ourselves to be up to the task of building and managed to raise substantial capital to continue growing the business and were now looking to scale up rapidly. We were in a position where we were getting healthier as a business as we were getting larger. To become better than what we were, we needed to invent and do things differently across many more segments of the business.

2019

(RE)BUILDING WITH COMMUNITY

Rishi and I were assessing the state of three of the pick-up vans that we had bought just a few months ago, despairing at the condition they were in.

Since we were delivering a lot of orders in vans at the time, we had decided a short while earlier to buy five brand new vans of our own. We wanted to see if operating the vans ourselves around the clock would be more advantageous to us than leasing them from third-party operators. The vans we were getting from third-party operators used to be very unreliable and would frequently break down en-route with grocery orders in them—either because they had not been maintained well, or had old tyres and mostly because they had probably crossed their real operating life a decade ago. They used to have a million or more kilometres on them (we only knew of this if the odometer was working) and were usually held together by innovative body work and the hopes and prayers of the drivers. That would cause us significant losses as a lot of products would go bad while the van was stationary on the side of the road.

Not to mention that we would often have vans failing to show up and complete their runs on time. More often than not, we had to keep more vans at hand than we required, and also not operate them fully despite paying for their time because we had no control over them. Our answer to our van woes was to start our own trucking company and buy some vans. We bought the vans with much fanfare, as our estimates showed that we could reduce our delivery cost by 30 per cent by operating them ourselves.

Except that here we were, within three months of owning our vans, staring at what looked like decades-old vehicles. The tyres had been swapped out for old retreads, the brand new batteries had been replaced with after-market second-hand knockoffs and every other possible part of the vehicles worth anything had been swapped out. The only hint that these were our months-old vans were the chassis numbers and their relatively shiny paint jobs. It was a tragic oddity and one that infuriated us as we examined the vehicles to figure out what all had been stolen. Meanwhile, the drivers had conveniently shifted blame from one shift to another, and, when pushed, had disappeared to look for other jobs.

All this meant we were nowhere closer to figuring out a way to reduce our cost of delivering.

Before 2019, we used delivery vans to deliver the orders that were placed on the app to the customer's doorsteps. Each van would typically follow a route in a certain part of the city and drop off orders at different customer's doorsteps. A typical van could deliver anywhere between twenty to forty orders in a day. This was a period where we didn't have as many orders and the vans would take time moving from one customer to the other. However, as our business grew, this dynamic started to change. Our vans were travelling less and delivering more orders, meaning that there were more and more customers ordering from us and these customers were close to each other. This should have been good for the cost of delivery, but that was not showing up in our numbers.

The vans were still constrained to carrying the same number of totes (crates in which orders were delivered to the customers' doorstep at the time). One van would leave our warehouse with, let's say, fifty totes and once all of them were delivered to customers, it had to come back all the way to the warehouse to offload the empty totes and pick up the next fifty. With the traffic in the cities and the distance to our warehouses, it was next to impossible to do this more than once in a day. So even though the vans were travelling less in the city, the overall benefit to us was negligible and capped at the number of totes that our vans could carry at once from the warehouse. Not to mention, since these were leased vans, we had very little control over whether the driver and the staff in the van had made any pitstops between their orders.

Totes (or crates) filled with customers' orders, ready to be dispatched from the warehouse

We knew that we had to do something that would help us reduce the cost of delivery as the volume of orders went up. At the time, a few people in our last-mile team decided to take an audacious bet—that of setting up the Grofers Service Partners (GSPs) network. The idea germinated from the fact that we wanted space somewhere in the city where we could store hundreds of orders to be delivered in any locality. The vans would deliver to customers from that storage instead of travelling all the way to the warehouses outside town. We would transfer the products from the warehouse to the local storage overnight in larger trucks. Doing so would reduce our costs and also give us more breathing room to provide better service and pass on some of the savings to the customers. A nice side-effect of this was that the overall emissions from delivery went down and the larger trucks didn't cause traffic congestion during the day.

However, as we set about looking for storage spaces inside cities, we realized we would need a lot of them and managing all of them by ourselves when we only needed them to function for a few hours in the day didn't make sense, both operationally and financially. We didn't want to pay rent for the entire facility when it would be empty for over fifteen hours in the day, not to mention paying for the staff stationed there. Some of our team members had experience in setting up operations for last-mile delivery networks in partnerships with local stores. So, we started going around town looking for businesses that could lend us some space for storage during the day. Our trucks would deliver the crates there in bulk overnight and our vans would pick up products from there in the morning and afternoon.

As we met more and more folks who either ran small businesses inside cities or just had space available, we realized that finding local partners who could store our products temporarily was not going to be a problem. Soon enough, we were working with a whole new category of businesses that had space available inside cities where they could store some orders for a few hours. Our vans would pick up the orders from these businesses and deliver them to customers. The project got off to a good start—we were paying these businesses per order to store the products from morning till the time the vans could pick them up, and we gradually saw an increase in the number of orders we were delivering with each van.

A key reason for this project working was that there were a number of businesses in the cities that had the same problem as us. They were paying rentals for twenty-four hours in a day but their business could not utilize the space throughout. These were small businesses like beauty salons, car repair workshops, real estate brokers and many such in the local markets that were happy to do a little bit more work and earn some extra money. A service partner would end up making about ₹6,000–10,000 per month and that was enough for a lot of entrepreneurs from the local market to want to work with us.

Soon enough, the partner network began growing on referrals alone and even more interestingly it started going beyond businesses. We started working with a number of women who were happy to sublet some part of their house to store orders and manage the inflow and outflow in return for earning some money while working from home.

Over the first few months of scaling this programme, we started to notice that more and more of our orders were coming from parts of the cities where the vans had trouble accessing the end customers. This was also in line with customers from hard-to-access areas finding our service more useful. They didn't have a supermarket or wholesale market nearby, so they appreciated the convenience of getting home deliveries of products. We needed larger spaces in these areas.

One of our partners, who used the ground floor of his family home as the storage space for our orders, suggested an interesting proposition. He was based out of East Delhi and his only source of income was the house in which he lived. It was built on land that he had inherited. His family lived on the first floor and he rented out rooms on the second and third floors. He had intended to rent out the ground floor as a shop but that had not panned out. Now, he was using the space to store our orders during the day, but he wanted to increase his income. Every day, when our vans would show up to pick up orders, he noticed that they had too many overlapping routes, which meant that sometimes one van would deliver to a certain area and two hours later another one would show up to pick up a different set of orders to be delivered to the same area as the first van. Sometimes our vans would show up one after another to deliver orders to neighbours. To him, it looked inefficient, although it was necessary for us to do as we promised the customers delivery at a particular time of the day.

The partner called up one of our people and proposed an arrangement. He knew how much it cost to deliver a single order to the area served from his storage using the vans. He proposed to deliver the orders for ₹5 less per order than what it cost us to deliver on vans and also offered to deliver in areas our vans couldn't reach. All we had to do was leave the orders at his place overnight and he would get them delivered during the following day utilizing his own workforce. Clearly, it was going to cost him even less to deliver and he could see himself earning the difference while still giving us a benefit of ₹5.

Now, ₹5 per order is a lot in businesses like ours. At the time, when we were doing 30,000 orders a day, it meant savings of nearly ₹50,00,000 a month. We realized that this could potentially work better for us and jumped at the opportunity.

The partners (whom we continued to call GSPs) stored the products and hired their own staff from their neighbourhood to deliver the orders, sometimes on bicycles, sometimes on motorbikes, and some even had a few three-wheeler autorickshaw drivers delivering larger orders for them. In fact, their cost of delivery was significantly lower than what we had been incurring by using vans. A number of small businesses had already been doing this for other e-commerce companies and sometimes only delivered one item per order—but we were now able to do this for our customers who shopped in bulk and ordered at least fifteen items every time.

An additional benefit of this transition was that the number of customers complaining about items missing in their orders went down significantly. In addition to selling parts of the vans they were driving, some enterprising van drivers had also been taking out easy-to-sell products from the customers' orders and selling them. It was very convenient for anyone to take a ₹250 brick of butter from an order and sell it to a roadside tea stall for ₹100. Now, with our GSPs controlling the delivery of products, they were able to keep track of who was leaving with what.

The project worked so well that we decided to implement it everywhere. Over a few months, we were able to stop using vans entirely and soon had a network of over five hundred GSPs across the nine cities where we were operational. The GSP programme was so successful for us that we became the industry leader in cost of delivery and were able to pass along significant savings to our customers. Not only did the cost of delivery improve, but we also saw our service levels improve. Not to mention, we could now get rid of the vans and not have to worry about the inefficiency or theft of van parts or of our products.

In a poetic flip, we had gone from being the hyperlocal delivery player to being a provider of goods dependent on a hyperlocal delivery network. Instead of setting up our own delivery, we had now created these hubs of micro delivery that were run by others. The one thing we learnt through the entire process was how finding solutions that required us to give up control sometimes went a long way in solving problems which were frustrating us and pushing us to go for more control. We wanted to own vans because the ecosystem did not provide us reliable working vehicles. Contracts, no matter how stringent, were often violated. It was nearly impossible to enforce any kind of penalties or lasting feedback systems to vendors to serve the quality we needed. Added to that, people barely ever thought about the consequences of committing petty acts of theft. Swapping out new tyres for old ones or selling some products from the delivery van was not considered a crime, but a smart way to earn something on the side. Everyone knew that the cost of going to the police to report these petty crimes was not worth anyone's while. At the same time, there was no moral right or wrong or social stigma attached to violating the law.

The moment the circle became smaller, social enforcement became possible. The GSPs were run by people in the same neighbourhood—not a faceless company. Suddenly, there was social stigma if you were called out for taking stuff from orders. Morality came into the picture because you were stealing from someone whom you saw every day. The law of the land got replaced by social policing that was built into the neighbourhood. A lot of the little things that had been frustrating us every day in our bid to scale up our business went away when we leaned on enabling the community to do the job and learnt to give up control.

Of course, working with partners had its own set of challenges. It was a learning curve for us to start working with the local entrepreneurs who joined our GSP network. First, not everyone we started working with was motivated enough or committed enough to be able to manage the supply chain. We had to get better at identifying the people who were going to run the GSPs themselves. We found that many of the people who wanted to partner with us were landlords who had spare real estate and were just looking to earn some money off it. Since they were not invested in the business or the space, there would be a lot of misses in the supply chain. Our trucks would turn up and the place would be locked or it would be left unsupervised and things would get stolen. We realized we needed to work with motivated entrepreneurs to do this and identifying them from the sea of inbound interest was hard.

Second, some of the best people who wanted to partner with us were not formal businesses. Apart from a few women who wanted to work from their living rooms, there were a number of informal small businesses like tea stalls, welding shops and puncture repair shops. They did not have GST registrations or Shops and Establishments permits to operate their businesses. This made it extremely hard for us to work with them. Over time, we established a process to help these businesses work with us and also scale with us in the formal channel. The owner of the tea stall under the Manesar flyover on NH8 was our GSP for over three years and eventually took a larger space across the road as orders in the area went up and his business with us grew bigger. In 2021, that former tea stall operator also started one of our first dark stores in Gurgaon for 10-minute delivery within Sector 52.

Lastly, the supply of goods into dense parts of the cities was and still remains a problem. While a lot of residential and mix-use development happens inside our cities, there is no provision for the efficient movement of goods.[1] These cities have only about half the road network required for the movement of goods. As our GSP network expanded, we had to keep investing in smaller vehicles to deliver to them within cities or choose partners in locations that were accessible to us but not close to customers. While we built a lot of technology to make the work of GSPs easier, we still ended up coming across physical constraints of access and infrastructure that were hard to overcome, no matter how creative the GSPs or we got.

Learning from these challenges enabled us to persist with building up the GSP network. Not only was it a better solution in terms of economics for us, but it was also a way for us to work alongside a lot of small entrepreneurs who helped us navigate the complexities of working in different neighbourhoods in the cities. In 2020, after the COVID-19 outbreak and the related shutdowns in the supply chain, it was this GSP network that helped us recover from the disruptions that the lockdowns and other restrictions had caused. As our warehouses slowly came back online in 2020 after the lockdowns were lifted, the GSP network was quick to scale up. It was heartwarming to see the level of initiative, as people overcame so much to serve their communities by making sure the supply of essential goods started at the earliest. The GSPs not only supplied goods, but also provided a source of income for a lot of folks hit by the lockdowns and disruptions to their primary mode of livelihood. I remember getting a message from one of the GSPs in Mumbai who operated a car workshop. He was enquiring if we could increase the number of orders that were passing through his facility as his staff needed to earn since there were no cars to repair. Stories like this from our existing partners and also the number of people signing up to become GSPs during the pandemic put pressure on us to do more. The fact was that even though there was enough customer demand, we just couldn't get enough people safely into our backend warehouses to meet it. With a lot of migrant labour moving back to their hometowns or villages and movement being restricted in the areas around our warehouses, we were not able to send enough orders from our warehouses to our GSPs.[2] However, this problem was about to turn into an opportunity for our organization.

Almost a month to the date of the first set of lockdowns, we were getting desperate and started working on converting our GSPs into mini-warehouses in the city. Since we couldn't get enough people into the warehouses that were outside of town, we decided to bring the warehouses to where the people were. We could move goods in bulk from warehouses to our GSP locations and all the work that needed to happen to prepare, pack and pick the orders for customers would happen at the GSP location. What started as an experiment to reduce the stress on our warehouses became an entirely new thing within the next few weeks. We got a store in the basement of a commercial office building and one of the GSP partners agreed to operate it as a mini-warehouse in Gurgaon. This became the genesis of what would later become the E3 programme internally—it stood for Express, Everything and Everyday Low Prices. Since the products were now inside the city, they could be picked and delivered within minutes. We started with delivering in forty-five minutes from the first dark store and realized that we were often much faster than that. The people delivering the orders were also collecting them from within the store and the GSP partner at the first store was enterprising enough to double the number of people picking and delivering almost every alternate day to keep up with the growing pace of orders.

Our first dark store being set up in Gurgaon in April 2020

We started reaching out to our GSP partners who had enough space and asked them if they would transition to this model. They would keep the products themselves at their locations and pick and deliver the orders. We would supply the products from the larger warehouses in bulk every night. Instead of paying the GSPs on a per order basis, we started sharing revenue with the partners and soon they came to be called 'merchant partners' in our system. To this day, the Blinkit mini-warehouses inside our cities are operated by hundreds of these merchant partners who eventually enabled the 10-minute-delivery model for us as well. A number of them had started working with us as GSPs back in the day and their business evolved with ours.

Notice that this business looked very much like the business that Grofers had started in 2015. Back then we used to show our customers the products that were available at nearby shops and deliver them from the shop to the customers. At the time, we were working with small businesses across a variety of categories and across the spectrum of sizes. We worked with small grocery stores like the neighbourhood kiranas all the way to supermarkets, bakeries, stationery shops, watch stores and almost any shop in the local market that agreed to showcase their products on our app. However, that business model had failed to scale.

We had faced two major problems with that business. The biggest was that stores that served walk-in customers as well were not able to accurately keep track of what they had in stock. The problem was different for small businesses and large businesses. For kiranas, the issue was that they didn't use a PoS to track and manage their inventory. Even when they did use it, they did not do so consistently enough for it to accurately reflect their store's actual stock levels. For instance, if the app displayed that a shop had two Dairy Milk chocolates in stock and a customer placed an order, our delivery partner might arrive to pick the order—only to find it unavailable at the store, either because the inventory had not been updated accurately or because they had been sold to a walk-in customer in the meantime.[3] In the case of large supermarkets, even if they tracked what was in stock, a customer carrying a product around in their cart within the store could still create inaccuracies.

The second issue that hurt the scaling up of the business was the general attitude of small and large offline businesses towards building an internet business. Small proprietors who operated stores in local markets wanted online business but primarily to sell directly to customers. They chafed at the commission rates we charged for bringing in customers and delivering the orders. They were happy to pay for a lead, but were generally reluctant to grow their online business if they didn't own the customer directly. They would frequently do things like calling customers up and asking them to cancel the order on Grofers and place it directly with them over the phone. Occasionally, some of them would also not prioritize the orders from Grofers because they were going to earn less from them after paying our commissions. There were also real issues for some of them—the online business generated focused demand at a larger scale. Some of the small businesses were reluctant to increase their inventory exposure or work in a more formal set-up to keep up with the needs of the online business. The ordering behaviour of customers online and offline was different and that meant stores would have to proactively manage the online business as an almost separate chain.

When we worked with large, organized businesses we realized that they had their own drawbacks. Even though they tracked their inventory better, it was not as accurate as we expected. More important, the online business would always be de-prioritized by them if there were more customers in the store. I remember the first Dhanteras in 2015 when we delivered silver and gold coins from local jewellery shops. Our delivery partners were told to wait for two hours by a shop in Ambience Mall, Gurgaon, so the shop could serve their walk-in customers first. No matter how much we tried negotiating with the companies to set up separate checkout lanes for us, inevitably the local store manager would always prioritize a customer who was in the store over one who had ordered online.

In order to overcome the challenges we faced in picking up orders from stores where customers also shopped offline, we started creating dedicated dark stores run by local store owners. That model was not successful either as we struggled to change how these businesses thought about running the store.

After 2015, we had given up trying to build a network whose supply chain was not controlled by us and were avoiding working with local players. However, the GSP network changed our view on working with local entrepreneurs completely. The big change we realized was that there was a huge difference when we were working with incumbents in business versus working with those who were looking to build a better life, and more important, were not suspicious of technology.

This is a big lesson in working with communities that we have learnt over the years. It is very difficult to get people in similar existing businesses to operate an online-first business. There is a reason they are successful in the offline business and changing those habits or ways of thinking is extremely hard. It made working with partners and communities that were already incumbents in local markets almost impossible—not just for Grofers but also for a number of businesses that have tried since.

However, folks in similar areas who have no background in running these businesses in the offline world have statistically been more successful in operating online-first businesses and partnering with us. I will share a few examples of the challenges faced and the data points that have helped to make this a very deep learning in my own thought process.

When our GSPs started opening up stores, they had no idea how to manage inventory or how to think about the technology bit of it. They were outsiders to this and, therefore, more willing to accept a new solution and learn along with us. The systems that were created when we started working with local partners who had no experience running stores or working in the retail sector were very different from the ones we were developing in 2015 when we were working only with existing store operators. In fact, in a case of déjà vu, we even onboarded a few FMCG distributors to open up stores for us in 2020 and realized that it was a mistake. It was way harder to convince them to do things differently—we were better off teaching a tea stall operator to run a dark store than someone who already ran a different kind of warehouse. Of course, there were some advantages to domain expertise as well but those faded in comparison to the advantages that hungry entrepreneurs with no baggage and an open mind to technology brought.

We knew that if we wanted to deliver faster and more accurately, we would have to innovate on how things were done in the stores and also in technology. The lesson we learnt was that for this kind of innovation to happen, we also needed local partners who were open to new ideas, and these could never be incumbents.

Local entrepreneurs grab opportunities in ways that are often different from the obvious ones. A famous example of this is how the distribution of mobile SIM cards was picked up by the next generation of FMCG distributors. Instead of operating in similar spaces as the parent business they wanted to be part of the next generation of businesses. As mobile telephony became bigger, those people who had a background in FMCG distribution were able to transition into successful distributors of SIM cards. The job might have been in a space connected to mobile telephony, but by and large the actual work was still very similar to the job of distribution. However, when technology intervenes and changes the way things are done, incumbents struggle to adapt and those with less or no baggage are the ones to adopt the newer solutions faster and in a more effective way. There is a parallel here when recruiting people for jobs as well. When start-ups are changing the status quo in a sector, assembling a team which has experience primarily as an incumbent might not work as well. People often find it hard to break mental models that they have spent years perfecting—and therefore struggle to solve problems using objectivity and first principles.

This does not mean that working with local partners was a breeze in this model. Just as in any other place in life, you come across good apples and bad apples. When we started opening stores that were operated by local partners, we came across partners who were genuinely doing this to scale up their earnings and were really invested in building a long-term business for themselves and their families. Every other day there were stories of how someone or the other had found a more efficient or better way to do things. Like the issues with our truck drivers, one of the most persistent problems we faced was that of theft of everyday items. Our inventory primarily consisted of groceries, which were extremely fungible items—meaning, one could always find buyers for them if one was willing to sell for cheap. This meant that anyone in the ecosystem could steal and resell the products for cheap. It was a good deal for everyone involved and no one felt bad taking money away from a 'large' company.

When we got local entrepreneurs involved, they were able to control these problems a lot better. Since they were more invested, the incidents of theft and pilferage decreased. Like I said before, people were less motivated stealing from somebody they saw every day. This all worked fine, until the partners themselves decided that they wanted to game the system. We would find cases in which the partners had swapped good products in the stores for bad ones and sold the good ones outside. We would also find partners sometimes utilizing store assets for personal use, like taking vegetables home for free or using the cash from the store for personal needs. In many cases, this behaviour was a natural part of people's thought process, which was to maximize their earning and worry only about the present, and not invest in building a business or a relationship for the long run. In other cases, it was just bad decision-making to shore up money for something immediate by selling the products in store and charging the brands.

Of course, working with local entrepreneurs and setting up systems for them is time consuming and hard to do—not to mention understanding the constraints and thought processes of a very diverse and different set of entrepreneurs.

The three biggest hurdles we had to cross in working successfully with small-scale businesses were educating them on the value of using our systems, convincing them and giving them the confidence to think longer term than the here and now, and, lastly, figuring out how their small business could access the much-needed growth capital when they became successful with us.

When it came to getting them used to working with our systems, we quickly realized that we had to meet them where they were, rather than expect that they would be able to work and act like the professionals who usually designed or operated these systems. Not all of them had formal education or a sound understanding of operations or finance. So our job became more focused on figuring out how to make things automatic for them. The benefits of operating a system like this included not only higher efficiency but sometimes also uncovering insights and implementing things that we thought were hard to do. For instance, we used to have elaborate handover processes when our trucks would deliver the products to our partners' stores. We had to do this because we were accountable for the accuracy of inventory to our sellers and our customers. To the partners, it just felt like a whole lot of work for no value. They thought they could just take a cursory look at the products and didn't need to record what they could clearly see. We realized that we had to both connect the stocktaking to something that mattered for them (which was usually payouts or costs) as well as build the technology that would actually make it significantly less time-consuming to finish the process. Instead of penalizing them for inaccurate inventory updates, we started incentivizing accurate updates. We figured we would save more money from accurate updates than we would spend on the incentives, and we did. We built elaborate data and tech systems in the backend so that we could do the exercise with minimal effort and without requiring any additional investment from our partners. Over time, these systems became the backbone of recording and scaling up the inventory movement of our products across the country's dark store network.

A much harder task was convincing local entrepreneurs to think long term. Like a lot of small businesses, their business is very much tied to their personal lives. It is the place where they have invested much of their life's savings to create a meaningful avenue of income that can fulfil their capital requirements. They easily became very nervous or edgy if it seemed like their earnings were about to drop or their investments might be in jeopardy. Occasionally, it also meant that they would lose hope and turn to siphoning off money because they thought they were going to lose their capital. While the latter was a scenario that happened once in a while, the former, where they would get nervous quickly and felt they had to do something to tackle even short-term losses, was a more dangerous thing for our business. Partners would frequently fire their people or downgrade their infrastructure if they felt they were not making enough money. In a tragic demonstration of this, one of our partners in Gurgaon was perpetually suffering losses because his inventory would go missing at the store. We initially thought that someone at the store was stealing things, so we investigated. The culprit item turned out to be frozen fish. We were intrigued because the losses from frozen fish were high and we figured no one individual was capable of consuming that much fish, nor was it an item that would easily sell in the market. We then discovered that the partner had instructed his staff to shut off the freezers at night when the store closed to save on electricity bills. However, turning off the freezers that were meant to operate around the clock meant that the fish in them would go bad and start smelling. The cleaners in the store would throw away the stinking fish every morning when they opened the store because of the bad odour, and the partner would incur more losses on the frozen fish—the exact scenario he was trying to prevent.

Over the years, we have provided various levels of support through programmes to help partners operate more like formal businesses, enable them to take the ups and downs in income in their stride, and identify issues and fix them. We have been somewhat successful in bringing about social change to improve attitudes towards running businesses for the long term.

One thing that we eventually did solve for our partners was providing different kinds of capital support. Over the years, as this ecosystem became more integrated into our operations, we were able to provide scale-up capital to a lot of partners. One of our GSP partners, who started with one store, now has twelve of them with us and has even diversified his business outside our network. We have continuously provided capital support to partners who have performed well with us so that they could open up new outlets and build larger businesses. It is nowhere close to the capital requirements for small businesses in the larger Indian market, but it is something we are only too happy to do, given our own experience in raising growth capital early on.

Learning from this experience, in 2023, we started reaching out to ambitious people in rural areas to set up sourcing centres for our business. We would provide them the tech, infrastructure and working capital to source fresh fruits and vegetables every day. In turn, they would be responsible for ensuring the quality and packaging, and ship these products to our stores. We had looked at Amul's system of sourcing milk from farmers every morning and realized that we could replicate a version of it. Today, we operate hundreds of such centres in rural areas to source our products and are now investing in utilizing this expanding network to bring high-quality organic produce to customers as well.

From not being able to work with local stores and entrepreneurs to now integrating local partnerships firmly within our business, the journey has been a learning experience for me. I think apart from the lessons around identifying the right partners and creating the right systems to leverage local entrepreneurship, I was able to build a belief that forging these partnerships was essential to overcoming India-specific problems, like haphazard infrastructure and unprofessional work ethic among untrained workforce.[4] One of the advantages of being a technology-first company is that we could build systems that helped organize this vast economy for the utility of our customers. The people who signed up and helped us create these networks were participating in this effort in their search for more opportunity. Even though concepts like franchising and dealerships have existed in India for a long time, and will continue to exist, this is the first time we can potentially utilize these partnerships in more than one way with the help of technology.

Take, for instance, the fact that we could automate the settlement of payments for different farming partners, delivery partners and our merchant partners in a matter of minutes and execute direct transfers via UPI for individuals as well. This kind of investment in technology builds trust within the ecosystem that encourages more people to participate. There are no regulations that can produce as wide an impact as the general motivation of hundreds of thousands of individuals seeking a better tomorrow.

This participative economy is powerful in creating the kind of opportunities at the local level that formal employment will never be able to match. When we employ a worker at a local level, we are often dealing with replicating a process or enforcing an implementation. However, when we are working with someone who is looking to build a business there, we create a hub of innovation and creativity that is looking to grow. Giving them the tools, introducing them to technology and backing them with resources sometimes creates the kind of outsized outcomes that we could never have comprehended. If you had told me in 2018 that our attempt at building GSPs would one day morph into one of the largest quick-commerce dark store footprints in the country and change our fortunes entirely within a five-year period, I would have called you crazy—and I would have been right.

While 2019 was a journey towards sustenance and growing our business rapidly, we were entering 2020 with some apprehension again. Our business had become much bigger, clocking nearly ₹200 crore every month, but there was a lot of competition and we were struggling to grow as quickly as we wanted. We needed to hit a certain scale to utilize our infrastructure and turn profitable, and we had tried using marketing as a medium for it. Entering 2020, we were more focused on improving our systems and reducing our losses. We thought it would be another year of efficiency but with the impending pandemic, which no one saw coming, things turned out very differently.

2020

THE VALUE OF PIVOTS

'How bad is it? Will we survive it?' asked Vikas Parekh, who represented Softbank on Grofers's board.

He was asking the question on WhatsApp after I had sent him a picture of our largest warehouse in the country in flames. A 2,00,000-square-foot building with products worth ₹30 crores inside it had gone up in flames within hours. Thankfully no lives were lost, but everything else was gone—the facility, the products, the machinery, the racks and the servers. When a twenty-year-old garbage truck parked outside our Kundli warehouse had blown its faulty engine, the resultant flames had quickly caught on to its contents of discarded cardboard, eventually spreading to the inside of the warehouse. The fire had taken only two hours to fully engulf and finish off the biggest ever investment in our supply chain, till then. That cold morning in November 2020, I had relayed the information to our board members.

At the time, it felt like a real body blow. After a long time, we had been feeling like we were getting somewhere and were in a position to control our destiny. Then that feeling of control literally went up in smoke.

Our largest warehouse in Kundli, Haryana, engulfed in flames

When COVID-19 had engulfed the world and brought supply chains to a halt, we had been hit too. For weeks, we struggled to get our operations back on and, even after we did, we had to contend with the fact that some of our decisions over the past year had left us with less money in the bank than we would have wanted. We got the time to set our house in order as, all of a sudden, the entire world had stopped working.

The surge in orders meant that all the fixed assets we had were now getting utilized, allowing us to focus only on problem-solving rather than worrying too much about getting to profitability. We had taken hard decisions in line with every other business at the beginning of the pandemic and outside of letting any of our people go, we had cut costs dramatically, including giving up office spaces, stopping marketing and even asking our team members to forego salaries in return for higher ESOPs so we could deal with the sudden uncertainty.

As supply chains had gone down early in the year, we had realized a big vulnerability in our networks—its dependence on small pools of workers near our warehouses. With migrant workers leaving for their homes in any possible way, including on foot, we were suddenly left with a huge demand but no way for our warehouses to fulfil them. This was when we realized that we needed to build resilience into our systems so that we were able to access a larger pool of workers. We did not want to be stuck in a situation where the disappearance of the limited number of available workers brought our warehouses to a standstill. The fact was that in our quest to build an accessible model of selling groceries to customers, we had adopted a model that was unpredictable. We had lost almost 80 per cent of the workers in the warehouse: they had either left for home or were not allowed to leave their villages for fear that they would bring back the COVID-19 virus to the village. While we had come up against resource constraints over the previous three years of delivering to customers, we had never completely shut down. This was the most extreme disruption we had seen in our supply chain, and it laid bare the fundamental flaws in how we had built it.

This disruption forced us to rethink the way we were trying to address the problem we had identified for customers. We were trying to serve customers who could not be served by any existing format of modern retail, like supermarkets, and who had to rely mostly on wholesale markets for convenience. When our supply chains got shut down we realized that a number of our growing pains were occurring because while our service was more accessible to customers and gave them great value, it was not predictable. The limited pool of workers closer to our warehouses meant that we frequently had to limit the number of customers we could serve. In non-pandemic conditions, this meant delivery times would increase from one day to three days or very rarely, even beyond that. However, during the extreme crunch of COVID-led lockdowns, with an even smaller workforce and customer demand higher than ever, we had to shut down our service because we could no longer take orders. Forced into a corner, a part of our reinvention was addressing the real reasons that value—and, by extension, modern retail—had largely remained inaccessible to a large chunk of India's urban population. When companies like Unilever had started door-to-door marketing of their products like Dalda almost eighty years ago, they had also inadvertently adopted the channel or medium of sale that has come to dominate India's retail landscape: the kirana store. In order to be convinced to adopt new products, Indian customers need a trusted face and the neighbourhood grocery store became that channel. Over the years, brands that could figure out how to build this distribution gained an advantage as the shelf space at the kirana became the most prized asset. This, combined with a mode of consumption at large scale—in smaller packet sizes—created a unique supply chain that was very hard to replace. The lower-sized and lower-cost products could only get to customers via this one channel—the kirana store. The kiranas were efficient with their cost and in-tune with the needs of their neighbourhoods, ensuring their continued success.

Once the Indian economy opened up for investments from abroad in the '90s, a number of successful retailers from abroad started making their forays into the country. They found local partners and started going about the job of building replicas of their large global supermarkets in India. Then they came across India-specific issues. The number of people, especially women customers, who had access to easy transport was low. Unlike a Walmart in the US, that customers could easily drive their car 5 miles outside of town to reach, retailers in India had to set themselves up where more customers could access them.

Local chains like Big Bazaar set themselves up in malls inside the cities. Different chains tried out varied sizes of stores at different distances from the customers—what are called multi-format stores in industry jargon. Eventually, DMart also came into the picture by providing great value at a reasonable distance from the customers. Apart from DMart and Big Bazaar, no one else seemed to survive for a long enough period of time at scale. Something was still off for the large-format supermarket business in India. Space within cities was expensive and going too far outside of population clusters made these stores extremely inaccessible.

Added to this, there were curious patterns in consumption. When retailers entered India, they assumed that the global pattern of consumers looking for bulk pricing would be a good proposition for customers here too. However, even consumers who were able to access large-format supermarkets, displayed only a limited willingness to buy too much in bulk. This was a result of two factors. One, the customers who were most attracted by the cheaper prices at these stores were typically not car owners—so the very act of carrying that many things back home was, and still is, a nuisance. Stand outside a DMart or any other discounting chain and you will see families struggling to stuff an autorickshaw with their bulk purchases. The three-wheeler's volumetric capacity is a real limit on the bulk purchase cycle. The second factor was actually the way consumers in middle India viewed their limited financial resources. They preferred to have the option of money in their hand, instead of spending it all upfront. They would buy just enough to get through a few weeks and not spend the majority of their budget at one go. They wanted to be able to cover some other expense, if the need came up later in the month. This is reflected in the fact that anytime there are EMIs available on products, you find customers who are perfectly able to pay for things in one shot, still overwhelmingly opting for EMI. It is one of the cheapest and most accessible forms of credit that customers get these days.

There was another lingering and more sinister reason floating around, which didn't get talked about much. All the different 'formats' of stores got thought of by different customers as 'not for me'. What it meant was, it was either too posh or too 'run of the mill' for them. There was a stratification in the way people were shopping for retail—if they did not see people like themselves shopping from that retailer, then they wouldn't be interested in buying from that store and spending time in the aisles, even if it had the products they wanted. Consumers associated the kinds of products and the format of retail with status. All too often would I be roaming the aisles of a supermarket and realize that there was a homogeneity in the class of people who shopped at that particular store. Even though multiple chains sold the same things that were consumed by customers across different classes, buying decisions were based on other factors such as perception, location or access rather than value, quality or taste. Over its thirty-plus years of existence since the liberalization reforms, modern retail has barely got 5 per cent of the total retail in India, with neighbourhood kiranas and wholesale markets still dominating the trade. The only highly profitable and sizeable company in the grocery space that has really thrived is DMart.

Penetration of organized grocery-led retail in India vs. other countries

Timespan to reach from 1-5%

Germany	na
France	na
Italy	na
South Africa	8 years
China	8 years
Russia	6 years
Malaysia	6 years
Turkey	7 years
India	na

India's penetration slower: 4 years to get from 1% to 2%

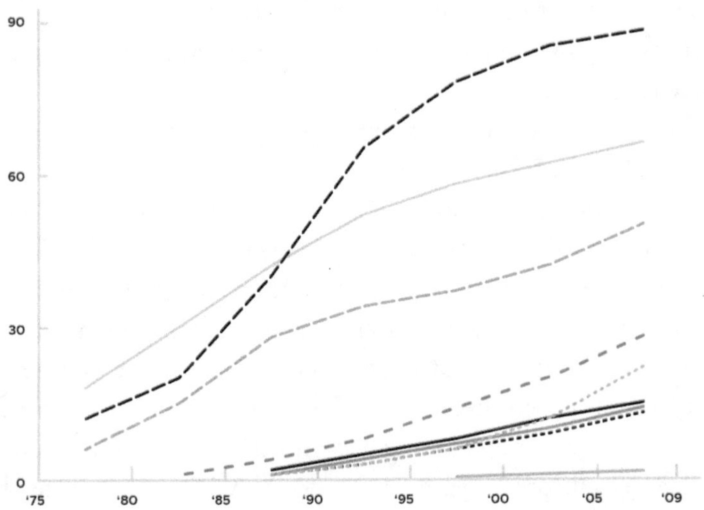

Source: Singhi, A. and Mall, A. (2011). 'Building a New India: The Role of Organized Retail in Driving Inclusive Growth'. Boston Consulting Group.

For Grofers, access, consumer behaviour and stratification of customers presented a different set of challenges. There is a well-known adage in retail circles, attributed to David Ogilvy: 'The customer is not a moron. She's your wife.' It is meant to make businesses and marketers realize that the person they work for—the customer—is not some unrelatable and mythical creature, but a real person making complicated choices. Except, what we were building at Grofers was not 'for my wife' anymore—meaning that we were building for a customer segment with which we were unfamiliar. We were all part of the car-owning, highly mobile group of customers who had no trouble accessing any form of retail we chose. On the other hand, Grofers was targeting women-customers from a socio-economic segment with limited access to value retailing.

When we started targeting more and more customers who did not have access to modern retail, we were really targeting lower-income groups and our ability to understand their needs and patterns of consumption was indeed poor. We made efforts to embed ourselves and understand how they thought but, at the end of the day, we were trying to follow them and not present a format that the customers would be attracted to. For instance, our service involved a trade-off between service levels and value. But because the service we were providing was unpredictable, it was harder for our target customer segments to decide whether we were their preferred shopping destination. Simply put, they found it difficult to compare the value of our service against other options.

What our data was showing us, and what we missed over and over again because we weren't attuned to the customer's way of thinking, was that lower-income groups sought value over service level. However, they needed to know clearly what that trade-off was—and it needed to be consistent. They were not going to spend their limited income in a place that was unpredictable—they needed to know if we were going to deliver in one day or in three. They hated uncertainty when financial decisions were involved. This was because the spendings they made were not from 'disposable' income. These were expenses necessary to run the household efficiently and if they had anxiety about us being able to serve them in a reasonable timeframe, they would choose not to spend on our platform, no matter the value we were providing. Even after overcoming their anxiety of shopping online and of getting enough value via lower prices, these customers wanted a standardization in the level of service.

This is where we were in May 2020. After having weathered the impact of the sudden shutdown of our supply chain, and the experience of bringing our warehousing back on track, we were now facing the realization that these disruptions were not a one-off problem—we had missed the larger weakness in our supply chain that was causing them. We had been losing customers without knowing it because of this problem even in non-pandemic times, and the large-scale shutdowns simply brought it front and centre. The chances that a similar disruption would happen again at a similar scale over the next decade were certainly non-zero. Even over a single month, there would be ups and downs that would make our business look unpredictable to our customers. The singular dependence on a finite pool of workers outside the cities was the largest factor we could not control, and that had led to this unpredictability.

It looked like we were sitting on a broken model due to the unpredictability of our operations once again. However, unlike the unpredictability faced in our operations in 2014, when we couldn't get our workers to follow a schedule, this time we were failing to even get enough workers to be concerned with the problem at hand. This problem of workforce shortage could only be addressed by having a presence in places where there was no shortage of workforce. No amount of automation could replace the need for some level of workforce in our facilities and this meant we had to figure out a way to relocate our most manpower intensive operations—the warehouses—to somewhere inside the cities where we would always have access to more manpower. We had to do this while not committing the same mistake that modern retail had committed over the last three decades, that of paying extremely high rentals in easy-to-access areas.

At the same time, we had to calibrate who our customers were and what we were offering them. Our ambitious new E3 project would entail opening mini-warehouses, again, within cities, adding as much of a selection as possible at the best prices that sellers on the platform could offer. We also figured that it should carry a service promise that we would be able to uphold all the time. Our first attempt at solving this was a hastily put together store in Sector 32, Gurgaon. Sitting in our houses amid the lockdown, we leased an empty godown in the area and decided that we would open a new format of mini-warehouses that would overcome, or at least mitigate, all the weaknesses of our existing model. The E3 project became a focus for me and a small team of people.

We experimented with multiple versions of design for the warehouses as well as how to operate them—not to mention how we would build the technology that would support all of this. The first store was a test bed for a number of ideas that either fell flat (like making the store an open format one that anyone, including the customers, could walk into and pick from) or really changed the way we did business (introducing on-demand gig work to our GSP partners). Over the next few months, we added an expanded fruits and vegetables supply chain, consistently started delivering in forty-five minutes and even started adding stores to convert the entire city of Gurgaon into an express-delivery model.

We also felt that the E3 format was starting to solve some of the problems that even modern retail had not been able to address.

It was a cheap enough proposition per order for customers—since the only variable cost was the cost of delivery—that it could compete on economics with the neighbourhood store. In a way, the customer was paying a delivery partner's cost of time rather than a neighbourhood shop's cost of location when they ordered. It was a small enough distinction, but it gave us the confidence that over the long term a better model could be to offer a larger selection with similar levels of accessibility as a neighbourhood store and the personalization of products for customers in different geographies.

We were also seeing proof of this happening. In lower-income neighbourhoods where we started opening stores, we saw customers starting to use us more and more for value packs and large-size products. In the premium localities, there was a focus on fresh produce, premium products and a wider range of personal care products. All of a sudden, this model also seemed to automatically solve for stratification as well. Faster delivery and a consistent promise were ensuring that customers were happy to shop from their homes, making decisions based on perception irrelevant.

More important, the average ticket size of every purchase started going down. While this isn't always good news for e-commerce and retail companies, in this case it was. What was happening here was that consistent and quick access gave customers the confidence that they could buy what they really needed for the short term according to what their wallet allowed. We started seeing this through an increase in the frequency of customers purchases, as well as a higher customer retention rate. Only occasionally did customers want to buy a few things in bulk, and they were able to do that when the need arose. At other times, they were happy to buy in smaller quantities and keep the money in their pockets. We had, unknowingly, created a third option that gave customers the flexibility that their neighbourhood shop gave them and access to the bulk-purchase pricing in supermarkets, and the product selection aligned a lot more closely with what the customers needed. This reflected in our growth in locations where we were opening E3 stores.

Over the year, we ended up opening twelve stores in Gurgaon and started converting the rest of the Delhi-NCR neighbourhoods to the express format as well. All of this was happening by working with local partners, like our GSP partners, who could operate stores in different neighbourhoods and also manage their workforce at a local level. The only support they needed from us was a constant supply of products from our brands, which is what our warehouses were now providing in bulk—with a much lower requirement of workers.

In the midst of all this momentum and optimism, the fire at the Kundli facility nearly took the wind out of our sails. Although I am not superstitious, it was hard to keep negative thoughts out of my head. Were we just unlucky, careless, or not attentive enough about our business? Why did every positive shift in momentum seem to come up against another challenge to be overcome? At the same time, the continuous expansion of our stores was proof that our organization was being pulled in a new direction all over again.

It felt like we were tantalizingly close to figuring out answers to the retailing conundrum in India. Mostly, we were able to get there by being experimental, nimble and, most important, resilient. The number of shifts in business models that we had gone through didn't give anyone outside any confidence that we knew what we were doing (and we didn't for the most part, to begin with). But by being open to moving ourselves in whatever direction we felt was best when we got new information, we had inadvertently been progressing towards creating a large opportunity. Even as events like the fire sent us into a downward spiral for a few days, the upward momentum from the green shoots of our efforts brought us back.

Such dramatic changes in the way of doing business are referred to as 'pivots' in business parlance and, more often than not, have a negative connotation attached to them. 'Oh, your original business did not work out so you ended up pivoting' is the general sentiment related to pivots. However, every single change in how we did some part of the business or evolved to find better answers were also pivots, albeit at a smaller scale. We were improving our business day in and day out as most businesses do, with small pivots, changing how we do the little things. Larger pivots would end up changing the nature of the business and its identity even more.

We were chasing one problem statement after another but doing that was also a way to sometimes be able to see the larger issues—and ways to solve them. Through our experiences in starting from a B2B platform, we had landed on a larger problem statement—the online ordering of groceries. We had been forced to move away from fast delivery as we couldn't make the economics work. By moving from stores to next-day delivery and moving to warehouses, we had discovered an underserved market for value in hard-to-access areas. When we had started solving this at scale, we had discovered the need for predictability even in this model, both for customers and our operations. That had now led us to a model that worked even better—our proposition of value, and the promise of fast and reliable delivery. We had come up with answers to larger problems and had ideas that could solve some of the issues that had held back organized retailing in India.

This time, we had set out to overcome the problem of resilience and predictability in our warehouses and, while searching for that answer, had landed on a model that addressed a lot of the shortcomings of what we were doing, and issues that the broader retail ecosystem and its value to customers suffered from. The increasing prevalence of stores, better feedback from customers and improved metrics in our system were pointing to a model that was superior to the one that had been the backbone of the company till this point—and one that we had spent the last three years working on. We were now gearing up for another pivot. These pivots had started to feel like a defining feature of our journey.

The value in our pivots and experiments did not lie in the ideas generated alone. It existed in the execution muscle, the resilience of our employees and the organizational humility in accepting that we were wrong and needed to go elsewhere. In a dynamic environment like India's, where the pace of change is dramatic, building pivots into the ability of the organization was an inadvertent side-effect of our journey, and one that would serve us greatly when we made the biggest pivot yet.

I believe these pivots are necessary in an ecosystem like India's, where large-scale problems are still unsolved. Pivots made by different organizations are probably the real-world equivalent of a laboratory conducting an experiment. Paying close attention to the different experiments of our own organization and tracking the history and underlying pivots that other organizations have gone through has given us the hope to create better businesses in an environment that is still in flux. In the business of inventing small systems or processes to improve our operations, I believe these pivots are not just inevitable, but necessary.

Even as most of 2020 was spent firefighting within our operations, and dealing with the pandemic and making sure our people and families were safe, we had also embarked on a path that would dominate our thought process about the future. We were entering 2021 with important questions: How could we ensure that we continued scaling fast deliveries, which seemed to be what customers needed, and how would we finance that transition? Little did I know that the events of 2021 would change Grofers in more ways than one.

2021

WHAT'S IN A NAME?

I pulled out my laptop and started typing a message to the entire Grofers team. I was about to change the direction of our organization. Again. Nervous yet fairly clear-headed, I sent the following message to the entire team:

> Effective immediately, we are shutting down our traditional online grocery business. From now on, every rupee, every resource, every waking hour will be focused on quick commerce. We will master ten-minute grocery delivery or we will die trying.

On our first day back in office after the COVID-19 outbreak in June 2021, I had drawn a line in the sand. We were changing direction. Grofers was going to be a 10-minute delivery company. That was all we were going to do and we were going to shut down everything else.

We had taken a measured call a year ago to start opening dark stores in the cities to overcome manpower shortages at our warehouses. Most of the stores opened in 2020 were growing and the quicker deliveries, happening in around thirty minutes, were doing phenomenally well. Now it was time for us to double down on the proposition, both out of desperation and a sense of opportunity.

While there was a certain level of optimism and fear around the success of quick deliveries, we had endured a lot of criticism back in 2015 when we used to focus on deliveries in ninety minutes—that the business was unsustainable and we had been wrong in trying something so foolish. However, seeing the number of express deliveries go up every day, there was a part of me that wanted to believe that this model would still make sense. More important, we had grown well as a business when we had offered faster deliveries in 2015. Customer behaviour had also clearly seemed to indicate that they were much more willing to transact with us if we were offering quick deliveries.

The first big question was, how quick?

At the time, our biggest competitor, BigBasket, had started offering same-day deliveries, which typically happened between six and eight hours of placing an order. When we looked at the numbers, those deliveries didn't seem to create any impact on how many more customers came to our platform or transacted with us. However, when we had started mini-warehouses inside the cities and started doing deliveries in forty-five minutes, we had seen an increase in the number of transacting customers. Added to that, offering fresh fruits and vegetables from these centres was also leading to more growth—something we had struggled to execute in our previous version of delivering the next day. A lot of the produce in next-day delivery would lose its freshness in the time it took to deliver from the warehouse to the customer.

Clearly, 45-minute deliveries were preferred over delivering in six to eight hours. Somewhere around the time when the Delta wave of COVID-19 was in full swing in April 2021, we had also tried delivering as fast as we could, which was typically in around ten minutes. At the time, we had converted our head office into a store to fulfil customer orders and were testing out delivering in ten minutes from there. We took inspiration from a Turkish company called Getir. They were in the news at the time for pioneering the quick-delivery model and taking it to different markets.

When we started delivering in ten minutes, it seemed that customers loved it even more than when we were delivering in forty-five minutes. Speed wasn't a feature anymore—it was the product. Deepi put it best at the time, 'Speed is the dopamine that this business needs.' After the Delta wave subsided in May 2021, I decided to figure out why the customers were loving the 10-minute delivery format. To my mind, the best way to study some of these things is to become a customer yourself. I asked the team to ensure that the store that served my house in Gurgaon was delivering all orders in ten minutes. It would cost us a little bit more, but I wanted to run with 10-minute deliveries as the primary service for a few days and understand why customers were willing to come back to it again and again.

After a couple of days of placing orders, I wasn't really convinced. My mom had made a passing comment that the quality of fresh vegetables seemed to have improved but apart from that I didn't register any big difference. Then one morning, while I was making coffee, I realized we were out of the cookies that we typically had with our morning coffee. I ordered the cookies on Grofers as I prepared my coffee, thinking they would at least be available for the following day. However, the cookies arrived even before I was done making the coffee.

At that moment, the penny dropped. The 10-minute service was something that fit into how people led their lives. I had forgotten to plan for cookies and the service saved the day. So, yes, 10-minute delivery made a lot of sense for emergencies or in last-minute-use cases. Those happened more frequently than we realized, but it still did not seem like it would sustain a regular or large business. While I was happy that I had got this insight, I wasn't certain about pledging the future of the company at the altar of 10-minute deliveries—until I saw my mom's phone.

In my household, my mom is the person managing most of the household needs. Although she wasn't very proficient in using technology, she had learnt how to use the Grofers app after I pestered her for years just so she could benefit from the convenience of the service. Like any proud parent, she was happy to do it but, like most Indian parents, was also super critical of everything. She would usually tell me when something didn't work or when she didn't like the quality or the selection.

That morning, after satisfying myself with the cookies and coffee, I joined my parents for breakfast. I told my mom about the cookies arriving in ten minutes. She said that all her orders had also arrived in a few minutes. Out of curiosity, I started going through the order history on her phone. In the week or so that the service had been live, she had placed a staggering twenty orders. Since I was never around at home, I had no idea that Grofers was being used so much in my own household. I started asking her questions about her orders. After scolding me for asking too many questions and not eating my breakfast quietly, she eventually explained her frequent orders. It was simply more convenient for her to get things as and when she needed them. It not only saved her trips to the market but also the emotional turmoil that goes with running a household.

In the past, she would get stressed if she ran out of something while cooking, or if she missed out on getting something that she had needed. It would necessitate a trip to the market with my dad or she'd walk there herself if she could. There was a store close to our house but it wasn't able to deliver all the time and had a very limited selection of items. The one that she preferred was about 2 kilometres away, and at most times of the day she had to budget at least an hour for the to-and-from trip—not to mention that she had to depend on someone to drive her there.

Listening to her, I realized that successfully managing a household, especially one like ours, where both my wife and I worked long hours, was fairly stressful. I had no idea that my mother had to go through so much trouble every day to make sure we had good food, our home was clean and well stocked. And this was when we had the privilege of living with my parents who were at home every day. If we were a regular working couple without a support system, things would get even more stressful.

In an eerie circular reference, that morning took me back to 2014 and the real reason we had decided to start Grofers as a customer-facing app. Soon after our marriage, my wife and I had designated Sundays as the day on which we would shop for our household needs. I hated the Sunday trip to the market. I wanted to be involved in running the household and not let that be my wife's job, but at the same time it was not the ideal way to spend our Sundays. The first couple of times it was fun to explore the shops and pick things for our house. However, over time, the hassles of finding parking, lugging our purchases to the car and dealing with long lines at checkout took away the charm of offline shopping. It had become a kind of drudgery. The answer at the time had been to change the Grofers delivery service into a customer-facing app from which we could order everything we needed from the same stores. Now, many years later, instead of that app being useful just for me, it was useful for my mom as well.

Suddenly, it all made sense. Our cities are developing and getting populated at a rapid pace, but they are not being developed in a way that fits the lifestyle of their inhabitants. For people like my mother, it was hard to plan for every possible situation, hence fast deliveries made a ton of sense. In a number of cases, the speed of delivery mattered even more. Delivering after one hour would also not solve the issue—for instance, new parents realizing their stock of diapers is over, guests arriving home unannounced, or running out of oil just as one is about to cook dinner. Some of these are cases where the only way a delivery platform can be helpful is if it can be as instantaneous as possible. With 10-minute deliveries, it seemed that we could transcend the inadequacies of infrastructure and services that made the everyday lives of people in our cities more taxing. From a company that was only solving for value in retailing, we could end up being a lot more for customers. We could be the answer to solving the everyday stresses that arose from managing and running a household.

This insight is way more powerful if you put it in the context of India. At that time, in 2021, with quick commerce proliferating globally, it was not yet clear whether it would work in India. There seemed to be a lot of capital flowing towards building quick commerce in other countries, including in China, Europe and America—but there was a general lack of understanding as to why quick commerce would be so much more relevant to India than in other places.

When we started delivering in ten minutes, for people like my mother and me there was a significant reduction in everyday stress. Errands that could easily add thirty minutes to an hour to the routine were now not taking any time at all. You no longer need to navigate chaotic traffic or poor infrastructure to get those errands done. They could potentially get done within minutes and without having to distract yourself from whatever activity you were engaged in.

As we set up more stores closer to customers to deliver in ten minutes, it was becoming increasingly clear that this model had found a market in India. Everything else we were doing in Grofers seemed like it was going to distract us from building this service. At the time, however, the rest of the business was not easy to ignore either. It was at a point where profitability was within reach. Whereas, on the question of quick commerce, the biggest issue was: How will it make money?

Early in 2021, the next-day delivery business was sizeable and doing sales of around ₹400 crore every month. In contrast, the quick-delivery business was only doing around ₹20 crore a month but it was growing much faster and seemed to have the potential to become a larger business. It was, however, extremely hard to convince our existing investors to bet on a six-month-old business that was likely going to cannibalize the larger business, which was closer to profitability and in which they had believed for a while. It was like convincing someone that the dream we had shown them was not good enough and now a new dream was better. In short, it felt like we were scamming them.

On the side, we were trying everything we could to raise more capital, including looking at a route to go public. At the same time, Zomato was also preparing to go public and in discussions with Deepi it was clear that they would want to have a play in the grocery space as their largest competitor was also investing in it. It was clear to both of us that quicker deliveries were the future. We had seen the rise of Getir in Turkey, which delivered a limited number of items in ten minutes, and wanted to see what would happen if we did the same at the scale of

Indian cities. I was focused on the promise of E3 and wanted us to figure out a way in which we could deliver value as well as orders quickly, while giving customers access to as large a selection of products as possible. This meant we needed to open larger stores and invest in much of the supply chain ourselves. The 10-minute delivery model coupled with our proposition of efficiency that delivered the best possible value for customers seemed to tick a lot of boxes that would help us reach a lot of customers. We were going to solve for trust, access, lifestyle fitment and value, all in one shot. For a company and its people who had been clawing and struggling their way to relevance and growth, it almost felt like a big moment of clarity. Everything we had learnt and experienced since the inception of Grofers was telling us that building this proposition was the way to go and all we had to do was find a way to make it work economically. Nothing else mattered.

This clarity, however, did not give any of our existing investors, or even our team members, confidence that the 10-minute delivery business would actually make money. The cost of delivering products faster was higher even though we were delivering from stores barely 2 kilometres away from the customers we were serving. The quicker delivery also required us to do a lot more capital expenditure in the form of opening more stores close to each other and close to the customers, across the city, so more customers could be offered deliveries in ten minutes. To add to that, when customers started ordering more frequently, as and when they needed the products, the average bill value of every order went down. So, there was revenue pressure. How we were going to make this model—with low ticket sizes, higher costs and an obvious customer need—profitable was not clear to anyone. The one thing we were certain of was that our experience in being a value-focused platform for the past few years meant that we had built technology and process expertise in the supply chain. If anyone was going to be able to operate this business with the lowest possible cost, we were confident it would be us.

There were a few other data points available to help us make this decision. However, looking at the size of the market in India and the fact that there weren't any businesses out there that addressed the India-specific pain points of customers in this space, we decided that going all in on 10-minute deliveries was the way to proceed. This was not all. We were also going to shut down next-day delivery completely.

As an organization, we were now desperate for success and we had enough experience to make taking brave decisions easier. The repercussions could wait—we were going to open five hundred stores before the end of the year. This was a big gamble. We were sunsetting a business that was doing over ₹4,000 crore in annual sales and going all in on a business that we had been doing for a little over a year. We did not have a strong plan for financing it, apart from the initial commitment from Zomato, but that didn't matter. We had to find a way to build this.

In my mind, it seemed like the only way forward. We had built up a lot of muscle over the years in technology, systems, supply chain and consumer understanding. All of that had allowed us to arrive at a proposition that customers were loving. It almost seemed like destiny that we had started with fast deliveries and built capabilities in the supply chain with a slow-delivery business only to come back to fast deliveries, but this time with better control on the supply chain, a greater selection of products and more value for customers—not to mention a lot more consistency. To a few of us, it didn't even seem like a trade-off. We had stumbled upon an answer that was way better for our customers than anything else we could offer, and we had to find a way to make it happen. 'Everything in 10 minutes' became a motto and an obsession internally. We had to do only those things that helped us to achieve delivering everything to customers in ten minutes or less. The part about figuring out how to finance it was my problem. But at the time, I could point the team towards a brighter future only if we could master the art of delivering in ten minutes or less. Finally, after the grind and effort of the previous eight years, everyone could see a glimmer of hope.

The hope came not just from our customers, but also from our own people. With every additional location that we opened with the 10-minute delivery model, more of our employees would report back on how it was changing their lives. They wanted to make the service better because it was creating a material difference in their own everyday lives.

While we ran the risk of all of it amounting to nothing, it was clear that if we did not act on this insight, someone else would eventually stumble upon it and make us irrelevant. In a nutshell, it was what is termed in technology circles as a 'product—market fit'—and eight years after starting the company, we undeniably had it. We just had to figure out a way to harness it.

Rational thought would have pointed to going after it at a more gradual pace. We had a relatively large business to operate, which was close to breaking even. We had proof that customers loved the new business, but limited knowledge about whether it would ever be profitable. Our decision to go all in on this new bet was a bit puzzling for outsiders. For me, though, it was the only possible path.

The biggest reason for choosing to do only one thing was gleaned from the lessons we had learnt in 2016 when we had tried to run two parallel services at the same time. During our first period of transition, we had split our mobile applications and the business into two verticals. One was the express vertical where deliveries happened in ninety minutes, and the other was the value vertical where deliveries happened the next day but the deals and product prices were more competitive.

In 2016, the success of the pivot to next-day delivery was still uncertain but we were hedging our bets that we would find answers to fix the problems of economics in our express vertical. Except that neither of the propositions grabbed the attention of consumers. If anything, presenting them with two different options confused them. The consumers who had started shopping with us were confused about not getting the same prices as the next-day delivery option and the value customers were surprised that the same items were also available in the express option but at a different price. In the end, many customers just threw up their hands and stopped shopping with us because they were genuinely confused. Recurring feedback we got was that they were there to shop and choosing options between business models was not what they wanted to put their minds to while buying products.

The value proposition had really started taking hold in 2017 when it became the sole option on the Grofers app. It was not just the app—we had to start aligning all our communication and experiences at the consumer touchpoints to demonstrate to customers that the platform's primary job was delivering value. There was a lesson in this experience, especially when you compared it to two phenomena that are observed outside of India but are not widely successful here.

The first phenomenon is the concept of super-apps. A single app on your phone that can do different tasks for you. In China, multiple apps have fought to become the go-to single app for everything, from shopping to payments to financial services and booking cabs and many more frequent-use cases. Some have even achieved that status, though to varying degrees of success. The logic in internet terms was that once you have spent money to acquire a customer who has downloaded and transacted on your app, it makes sense to offer them as many transacting opportunities on said app. The typical term used to describe the total transaction volume of a customer who is being chased in this environment is Life Time Value (LTV) of the customer. Apps try to maximize how much customers will spend on their platform as that is the path to increasing the potential profits the platform can earn from these customers by providing multiple products or services.

The second phenomenon, visible in the American market more than anywhere else, is an offline equivalent of super-apps, that is, the 'platformization' of connected services. What this means is that a single platform is trying to cater to the entire life cycle of the customers' needs. Take, for example, the case of Sears, the first retail company to IPO in America in 1906. Once they had started establishing their stores across the country to sell all manner of products from dry goods to fashion and appliances, they made their walk-in stores centres for different connected tasks related to the purchase. If you entered the store in the heyday of Sears in the 1980s to buy a washing machine, the appliance on offer could be from a brand that they owned, called Kenmore, which made its own line of appliances, and you could also get credit for the purchase. Across the billing till, along with banking services for the purchase, you could sign up for insurance via Allstate, another business owned by Sears, and if you wanted to buy a house in which to put the washing machine, you could visit a Coldwell Banker real-estate agent with an office in the same store, or if you so chose you could invest the money with a Dean Witter agent seated a few steps away. Coldwell Banker and Dean Witter were, of course, businesses that also belonged to Sears. This, in a nutshell, was platformization—one location catering to all your needs and possibly able to offer better value because all the different parts of the value chain are housed under one roof. Even today, businesses like Costco and AutoZone provide multiple services for customers under the same roof in what can be considered a modern version of the Sears platformization strategy.

Super-apps and platformization are essentially the same play across different generations and different touchpoints. While you still see vestiges of the offline platformization in some of the Western markets, its prevalence has reduced as specialists in every segment have sprung up to compete and laws around anti-trust and monopolization have become stronger. Not to mention that the regulatory advantages enjoyed by some businesses have disappeared.

While super-apps continue to be successful in some Asian markets, they have not been able to enjoy the same level of penetration or success in the Indian market. A similar pattern played out in the platformization efforts by many players across different offline categories as well. Cross-selling of services or value propositions have not been particularly successful in many sectors in India, online or offline. Even though some large conglomerates have lent their parent-name to multiple businesses to generate trust in smaller businesses, platformization has not seen much success.

The reason that super-apps and platformization have not worked so far in India is the nature of customer's association with a brand providing solutions to a specific problem for the customer. Indian consumers are attuned to building a relationship with a brand based on the problem it solved. If you look at the journey of brands in developed markets, you will see that when societies were developing, a lot of the stronger brands ended up becoming verbs in the parlance of customers. Brands like Kleenex, Hoover and John Deere came to represent the problem that they solved. You didn't vacuum the house, you hoovered it. A similar thing happened later with Google and the act of looking up something using a search engine. Closer home, Surf, Whisper, Pampers and a number of other brands came to represent the line of products more than just a certain product. Customers in India are still attuned to this way of thinking and trust in specific brands is paramount. This also arises from what the brands have taught customers over the years through their act of brand-building. Advertising and the messaging from large brands conveys a certain use case and lends the brand an element of credibility. This phenomenon does not just exist among brands that consumers buy, but also in products that are very different. If you have ever wondered why muscular Bollywood actors are often featured on hoardings for construction rebars that you have never heard of, it is to give distributors the confidence that they are dealing with a large, trustworthy company. Essentially, brand-building activities are meant to instil in customers the confidence that the brand will be able to do the job as promised. Surf will take out stains, Colgate will whiten and clean teeth, and so on. In a society that already lacks trust across the spectrum, consumers are being asked to trust the brand to provide a certain utility or service. Therefore, when a brand isn't saying anything specific and is a singular platform for many things, the customers are not entirely comfortable. This is the lesson we had learnt from trying to be two different things within the same app back in 2016.

In a funny way, even trust in public-sector institutions has a part to play in it. Whenever I have visited retail stores in Europe, I have noticed a very large number of products with brand names I have never heard of being sold in chain stores. They might be private labels of retail chains or smaller regional brands selected for their price or specific appeal. However, the customers there are confident in buying those products since their faith in their institutions is very strong—they know that if it shows up on the shelf, it meets quality standards. That is not the case in India, yet. Here, across product lines and types, trust is earned by brands over a long period of time through performance, communication and repetition of their message about what they stand for.

A combination of these observations had taught us that consumers in India preferred to deal with a brand according to the single proposition that the brand promised. In general, a 'sub-brand' approach with a single brand lending its name to unrelated product categories did not seem to work. As we became more and more certain that our future lay in 10-minute delivery, it also brought up the uncomfortable question: Could the Grofers brand change its identity yet again and start standing for quick delivery and peace of mind? We knew we did not want to create a dual proposition like we had in 2016 and confuse our customers. There was an element of financial expediency as well—we did not have money to start an entirely new brand and operate Grofers. We also wanted to break the association that our customers had with the Grofers brand, as it stood for value and good prices. We wanted to stand for speed, first and foremost, followed by selection and value. And so we went all in on the quick-delivery business.

In about six months, we became reasonably certain that our pivot was working—at both the operational and organizational levels, and with the customers as well. That was when we decided that the best way for us was to lean heavily on the new identity of a quick-delivery company, and come up with a new name. This time around, though, the decision was not as simple as saying we will build 'whatever' brand we want. Now that we were set to replace the Grofers brand, which already had some salience in the minds of customers as a value-first e-commerce platform, we needed our new identity to communicate the nature of our new value proposition—speed.

After a few checks on the available options, we settled on a name that communicated the instant nature of our new pivot—we decided to rename Grofers to Blinkit. The name change happened exactly eight years to the day we had launched the Grofers consumer app.

The day we changed our name from Grofers to Blinkit

The decision behind changing the name wasn't just tactical. It went back to the question of consumer trust. We wanted to adopt a new identity as an organization as much as we wanted to shed the old one we had invested in. While we had to invest a significant amount of our remaining bank balance to effectively tell the customers that we were changing our name, it was not a one-off process. We also had to change our different consumer touchpoints to reflect that we were a brand that now promised faster delivery.

The most important impact that we were able to achieve with the rebranding was in the ways of working and attitudes of our internal team. As much as we had to build our brand identity to talk about speed, convenience and peace of mind for our customers, our teams changed their way of thinking about the problems when we changed our name. The way of thinking about serving customers moved from the 'Grofers' lens to a 'Blinkit' lens. We could carry forward our knowledge and experiences while building an entirely new company and not be weighed down by past decisions.

In a rather interesting parallel, back in 2015, we had been hit by a number of frivolous lawsuits against our name when news had broken about a large round of capital we had raised. As it was my first brush with trademark law in India, I had reached out to our law firm to help out with the flurry of activity around our brand. The partner on the call had laughed, saying that it was a rite of passage to get hit by such lawsuits—in his words, it was a signal that we had arrived. While I didn't totally buy it at the time, I had to repeat the same words to calm down our nervous legal team this time around when we were hit once again with a bunch of frivolous lawsuits only a few months after renaming ourselves to Blinkit.

The decisive pivot to 10-minute delivery seemed to be working, but it would still take the act of scaling up the business over the next year for us to really figure out why it was successful. It was not just the consumers and their needs, there seemed to be a large correlation between how our home lives, work lives and our cities were interacting. The impact was not just visible in our business, but also made sense when we figured out what it meant for our people.

2022

THE OPPORTUNITY IN OUR CITIES

I was visiting one of our stores in Madhavpura, Bangalore, and decided to deliver a few orders with our delivery partners. One such order really stood out for me—both in terms of the impact our business has on people and the future that we need to build for our cities.

The order had been placed from a small society close to the store and I reached the location riding pillion on the delivery partner's bike. I rang the bell of the apartment on the first floor. The delivery partner had delivered orders to the same house before and greeted the customer, explaining to her who I was and that I wanted to talk for five minutes. She was a young mother and had a one-year-old, who was on a bed next to the sitting area, which was in the same room. The apartment itself was a one-room studio not more than 200 square feet (due to the nature of my work, I have picked up the annoying but uncanny ability to tell the size of rooms that I am in).

The lady was extremely polite and warm. She was hesitant to invite us into the house, so she left the door open to talk to us without really letting us in. It worked for me, as I wanted to understand more about why she was a customer of Blinkit and the problems we solved for her. She was extremely generous with her time and thoughts on all of it.

She had moved to Bangalore three years ago after getting married. Her husband was a project manager in a construction company and had moved to Bangalore from Assam a few years before she had. It wasn't an affluent household, but one that was building its life and its own story. As her husband worked during the day, she relied on Blinkit for whatever she or her child needed. Earlier, she used to send a message to her husband and he would bring everything on his way back from work, but she realized that it caused him anxiety if he could not leave work in time.

The real clincher for relying on our service was the low level of accessibility to the products she needed close to her home. As the road leading to her society was a dead end, she had to walk at least 350 metres to get to a place where she could hail an electric rickshaw to get to the closest set of shops, which were maybe a kilometre from the house. She could neither take the child with her nor leave the baby behind and go by herself. Earlier, she would go to some shops nearby, but they were built on encroached land and were demolished, only to open up on the other side of the busy road. Now she had to cross the road and navigate traffic to get to them. In the end, she chose to use Blinkit because it was the most convenient option for her and safer, because she didn't like the idea of crossing a major arterial road that had no facilities for the safety of pedestrians.

As grateful as I was to hear about the impact our company had on her life, it was also a sad reflection on accessibility in one of our largest cities. If the design and development of our cities happened in a human-centric way, it would limit the frustration, exhaustion and effort of citizens as much as of the people who create the services, technology and products that spur development.[1]

In a way, we are choosing to live in our cities in the same way as our supply chains function—through brute force. I am not sure, for instance, how I would be able to manage my life in Gurgaon without the benefit of a driver, a cook and a cleaner (for many others, who can afford it, this list would include a dog walker, a nanny or other kinds of help). These services are available today because there is a big enough labour pool that is keeping cost of these services low. Ideally, the providers of these services should be doing more productive jobs, and the city should be friendlier for me to live in so that the services and products I need are always accessible. These are jobs that add to other people's productivity, but are not considered 'productive' in the context of the country's economic development in themselves. As the gap between labour supply and demand tightens, access to these exclusive services will become harder; this is already demonstrated by the increasing level of wages for these workers. The lack of easy access, and in some cases accessibility on the whole, to basic life requirements is also the reason for the increasing acceptance of at-home services, like the quick delivery of groceries or salon or cleaning services. As more and more people find alternative employment opportunities in manufacturing or gig work or even opportunities closer to their homes and villages, the supply of cheap labour will also reduce. This will further decrease accessibility to easy personal help and push people to seek more services that do the same job.

Why quick commerce was working for us as a business and why it made sense to customers started becoming clearer to me as I processed this experience. One of the advantages of running a physical and operationally intensive business is the ringside view that you get to the daily lives of customers. How they adopt or reject certain services depending on their needs and the alternatives available to them can only be understood when you attribute their choices to their environment. For our customers their environments are their cities, and I realized that quick commerce was being adopted because the cities we live in are unable to keep pace with the expectations of an increasingly upwardly mobile population.

For start-ups and companies being built to cater to our cities, our workplaces, cities and services becoming seamless and accessible is a positive compounding loop that has failed to keep up with the pace of urban growth. Our cities are the best centralized bets for the delivery of essential services to customers. Across the board, whether it is healthcare, education, employment, childcare or upskilling—we have a large divide in the quality and volume of such services available to the top 1 per cent versus the rest. With cities growing bigger and more people concentrating in them, there is an opportunity to deliver higher quality experiences to these populations—something which wasn't possible forty years ago with the majority of the populace inhabiting smaller towns and villages. However, the gap between people's needs and their ambition and the reality has only been increasing. And whenever the existing amenities in cities are not able to deliver to the expectations of these services, it creates opportunities for businesses to fill that gap.

If you are ever at IFFCO Chowk in Gurgaon, or on the highway (not just around there but right on the highway itself), you will see a number of people standing on the side waiting for a passing car to take them to their destination. They are carpooling with people who are looking to use their cars to offset the cost of their commute. At the same time, drivers with empty cars also use this opportunity to make some extra money on the side. All of this is unregulated, untraceable and potentially unsafe for commuters—especially when you see seven people in a car meant for five or overburdened two- or three-wheelers chugging along at 25 kilometres per hour on a highway meant for vehicles operating at 80 kilometres per hour. The fact is that everyone providing these services—whether a private car owner, a driver with an empty car or a three-wheeler driver—is doing so to earn a living. There is a business opportunity in the absence of formal services, and these folks are simply stepping in to fill that gap. None of the people taking these dangerous rides can afford a taxi to work every day but there are no alternatives available to them. The only way one can take public transport to cover the distance from the highway in Gurgaon to the highway exit close to the Indira Gandhi International Airport in Delhi is by changing two buses, which run at intervals of an hour.

Over the years, I have seen different kinds of entrepreneurs take a shot at solving this problem. Apart from the small-scale, informal businessmen providing transport services on highways, there are shared bus services like Shuttl and City Flo and the first wave of bike taxi companies like Baxi. Almost all of them have been shut down by regulators at some point or the other. Now, the regulators might have their reasons, but to shut down a service that was trying to provide an on-demand, technology-led, traceable and safer solution for a basic daily need does not seem progressive. In fact, it is ignoring the very solutions which are trying to fill the gap between what people need from their city's environment and what the city is able to provide.

This puts the productivity of a lot of people at a disadvantage. For work commuters, the comfort of a shared bus with an assured seat was replaced with yet another period of standing on the highway and thumbing their way to the office, hoping to reach in time. The reason this is an important issue to address is that the pace of innovation and work that organizations operating in these cities can accomplish is almost entirely dependent on the quality of its employees, the level of their motivation and their mental health. If our resources show up for work after an exhausting two-hour commute in the morning, it is unlikely that they will be able to compete on the global stage in the knowledge economy.

This impact of our urban environment on worker productivity does not address the other, larger issue—the above-mentioned 'options' are even less viable for women. Almost all the people getting into these cars are men—they are the only ones with the ability to access an unregulated form of commute because there is no other option. In my view, we cannot expect willing participation from women in the workforce and utilize their talents for development till we actually take care of these things.

In 2016, when our office in Gurgaon used to be in Sector 32, it was close to an old village, a pocket of Jharsa. The inhabitants of Jharsa were rural folk primarily existing on cattle economy and some agriculture until the the '80s, when Maruti's first plant sprung up and, subsequently, DLF started setting up what would become metropolitan Gurgaon in the late '90s, in lockstep with the BPO boom. Soon the small canal close to Jharsa disappeared into encroached land and the village itself became a hotbed of untoward elements, all looking to grab a piece of the land that was now worth a lot more than many of its original residents would have thought. The messy nature of land records and ownership meant there were plenty of fights and feisty encounters that helped the place become an active focus for petty crime.

This place was around 100 metres from not just our office but the offices of Google and several other organizations. Some privileged citizens who worked in these offices had the option of rolling up their windows while their chauffeurs navigated the area. Others had to make their way through it on their bikes or in their cars, but we advised them to avoid the area later in the night after a couple of untoward incidents. Then there were those who were dependent on public transport. Their privilege levels determined their access to the safety that our cities could offer. Many employees had no choice but to get off at the nearest metro station and commute the last mile in autorickshaws, especially late at night or early morning when our office shuttles were not functional.

One day I got a rather alarming request. One of the leaders of our customer servicing team requested that we move all the women to afternoon shifts. Worried that I had missed an incident, I asked for details. I was told the request had been raised because the local government had recently banned bike taxis. Now, I had read in the news that bike taxi services had been banned due to protests from autorickshaw unions. These service shutdowns affected the ability of our employees to get to work easily. The women in our office who were commuting via metro used to find it safest to take a bike taxi from the metro station to the office as they were in plain sight during the day. It made them feel like they had more control on their environment and security. They didn't have the same level of comfort in a shared auto, especially since their co-passengers were almost always men. Not only was the bike taxi cheaper for them, it was the safer option. With one rule change, an entire industry got wiped out (temporarily, though we did not know that then) and a major source of convenience and enablement was taken away from the people who needed it the most. Some of the women in our office had chosen the job because they could map out a safe route from their home to our office building, and the bike taxi was a crucial part of this commute.

Of course, it is unfortunate that we have to worry about women's security to begin with. However, if we are not going to be able to influence the larger society, we can at least expect local governments to work towards making life more manageable for their citizens. The unfortunate impact of these developments is that it puts opportunities (and willingness) to contribute to the workforce further out of reach for women. For early-stage companies, it reduces the pool of capable people to choose from and also impacts the productivity of those whom they do choose.

This is a story that plays out every day and one we need to deal with. The safety, security and well-being of our workers should not be subject to their backgrounds, income levels or gender. Since the systems are failing to offer solutions, especially to people at low-income levels, daily inconveniences are the first things that people try to solve when they become upwardly mobile. The shared ride on the highway gets replaced by a scooter or a motorcycle (somewhat safer and within one's reach) or perhaps a car because citizens are getting the message that they have to do something about their own problems. The promise of a metro line by 2037 doesn't help them solve the issues with their daily commute in the present. Meanwhile, everyone is wondering why traffic is worsening and the roads are more choked than ever. It is happening because there is no alternative. Everyone is merely trying to change their everyday lives for the better—by choosing outcomes that are making things collectively worse off.

To prove this point, we tried to find out the average commute time for our human capital. The results point to another problem that is both large and unacknowledged despite showing up clearly time and time again—our daily commutes and poor travel times are a drain on everyday productivity. The average commute times and average distances are not measured anywhere in our urban planning or city design constructs, and even if they are the process is fairly unscientific. For instance, our road plans are built over multi-year masterplans for the cities. Whether a road is 30 feet wide or 70 feet wide is determined by the estimated increase in population over the next few years.[2] That is, the expected population that is supposed to use this public utility. However, this planning does not account for a crucial piece of technology advancement. Almost everyone on the road is using maps. So, all the roads in the cities are now part of a network accessible to everyone. If you have ever been to Bangalore, you will have faced the frustration of sitting in a cab being driven through narrow village roads because the main road was choked and the map switched over to a less congested route that goes through heavily populated areas. All of a sudden, roads that were meant to be accessible only to pedestrians or at best to two-wheelers now have intra-city traffic moving through them. Not only does it bring human elements in contact with a vehicle not meant to be there, but the resulting jams and chaos are enemies of efficiency and progress.[3] This, coupled with the fact that we still view urban transportation through the lens of solutions invented a hundred years ago, whether it's the metro, bus, car or the road itself, tells us that we are not bringing the best available tools to the problems at hand. If we allowed more innovative solutions to take hold in our urban environments, there could be solutions that leverage the technological advancements to deliver superior services, rather than making this just the government's problem.

Here is the estimated population increase of the Delhi, Mumbai and Bangalore city areas over the last two decades.

Estimated population increase in Delhi, Mumbai and Bangalore over the last two decades

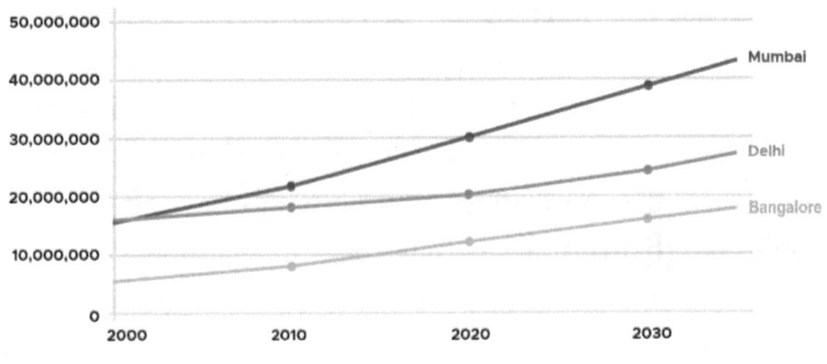

Source: United Nations, Department of Economic and Social Affairs, Population Division (2018). 'World Urbanization Prospects: The 2018 Revision, Online Edition'.

As seen above, a lot of people are moving into these cities. People who will need things, who will occupy living spaces, who will travel to work and who will own vehicles. They will also need healthcare services and schools and a functioning retail economy. Our cities are demonstrably at a point where they are far behind the pace of expansion and development and the ever-increasing aspirations of their inhabitants. This despite the fact that a lot of effort is being put into infrastructure and forward-looking development in these cities.

The vicious cycle here is that investment in singular infrastructure like roads will lead to even more vehicles on the roads, causing more pollution and the outward spread of the cities.[4] In core areas within our large cities, we are increasingly becoming heat sinks as green spaces are being taken over to build more roads, apartments and offices.[5] In effect, we are seeing the chaos and pains of a rapidly developing nation. Arguably, one of the largest existing casualties of this lack of infrastructure is the quality of life of our human capital.

When we, as a company, started making the shift to quick commerce and the 10-minute delivery model, the fact that the service was used so much by so many people surprised us at first. It was only when we started digging into the daily lives of our customers that we realized that they were choosing this solution to make their everyday lives better. If something is saving the customers the hassle of interacting with sub-par infrastructure, they will take that option in a heartbeat. We can bet on the fact that our cities will get bigger and there will be a need for more housing, infrastructure and services. However, the way in which they expand and the environment that organizations or even governments get to invest in the future is still quite fuzzy. A number of services, like quick commerce, will need to flourish in different parts of our cities to fill gaps that our infrastructure cannot adequately cover. There is a case to be made for allowing these services to innovate and expand if these problems are to be solved at an unprecedented scale.

Delhi-NCR has become a behemoth with multiple massive hubs of commercial activity and residential development. To demonstrate the scale of the challenge of traversing the city, I will illustrate what it takes to operate a supply chain business in Delhi-NCR. We are dealing with three states, multiple districts and the resulting chaos of conflicting regulations in each of these places. Delhi does not allow the entry of commercial vehicles beyond a certain size during particular times in the day. The rules are different for Noida, Ghaziabad, Gurgaon and Faridabad. Zoning regulations related to building warehouses are again different across the three states, as is the quality of infrastructure available, where the development of supply chain infrastructure is even allowed. A combined metropolis of over 30 million people and over 6 million households must be supplied with everyday essentials. But the movement of goods is subject to widespread, systemic inefficiencies, leading to inferior service quality and higher costs for the end customer.[6]

Higher prices of goods for end consumer due to fragmented supply chain

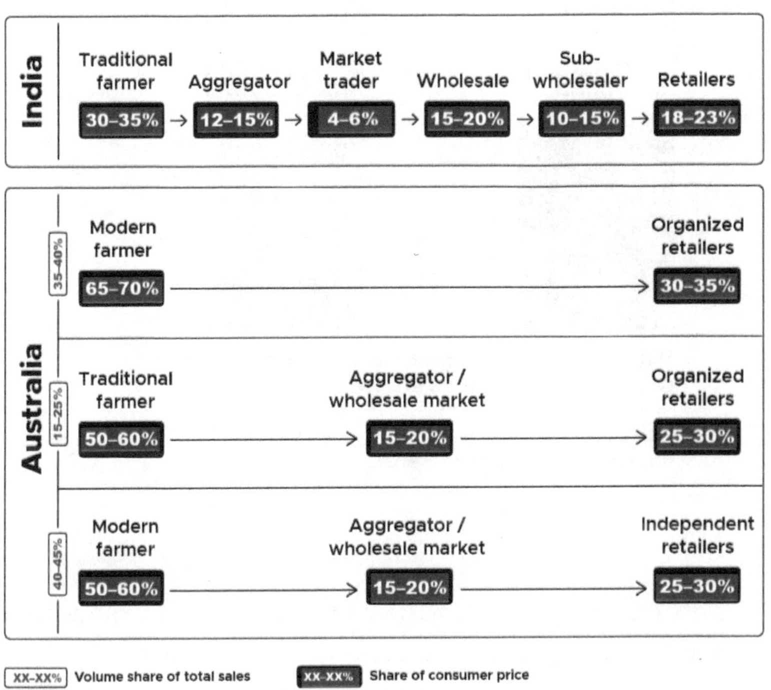

Source: Singhi, A. and Mall, A. (2011). 'Building a New India: The Role of Organized Retail in Driving Inclusive Growth'. Boston Consulting Group

High indirect or 'hidden' costs due to India's fragmented supply chain

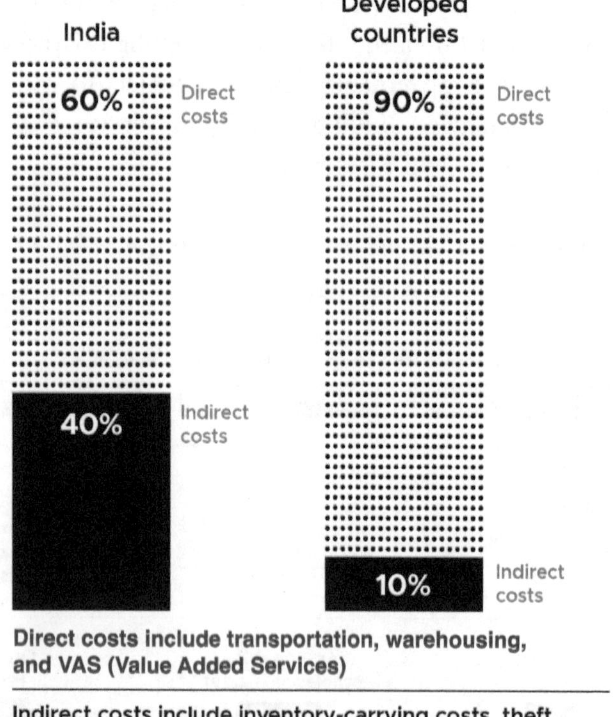

Source: Kuruvilla, T. et al. (2020). 'Reimagining India's Supply Chain'. Arthur D. Little

This creates a massive barrier for future investment as well for services businesses like ours, because we do not know how the individual regulations will change over time and affect our business. Maybe the warehouses we open today will be condemned tomorrow or the facilities we choose today will become uncompetitive tomorrow because the underlying parameters on the basis of which we chose to invest will have drastically changed. Today, if Delhi changes its policy on vehicle entry into the city, our entire Delhi-NCR network will almost certainly drop significantly in efficiency. There is often a conversation around the impact that a systematic regulatory environment can have on growth and development or the process of building an organization. There are large-scale national-level regulations that are talked about. However, in everyday life, the mesh of local rules and regulations not being aligned to a broader perspective of growth and development creates negative pressures that really hold back this development. Local priorities smother the ability to build things that are needed for the greater good.

The COVID-19 pandemic was a stunning and tragic illustration of just how dysfunctional things can become. One of our facilities at the edge of Delhi-NCR was not allowed to open due to the lockdown even after grocery delivery had been marked as an essential service. Most of the people at Grofers at the time were moving between different offices of government to solve the issue, while staying away from their own families to keep their families safe from contagion. I was isolated in a room in the house because I had to go out every day and didn't want to bring back the virus to our household, to my grandmother, my parents and my wife.

Amidst all this confusion, there was still a spirit of cooperation between government officials and our people. At the end of the day, the government officials on the job were also risking the safety and well-being of their families to navigate the chaos. The problem was that orders and directives were being interpreted by different people differently. So, while we got the order to open our warehouse to start the essential service, we had no workers at the facility. Most of the workers in the facility (nearly four hundred of them) were locals who came from the villages close by or were migrants who had found accommodation in the nearby villages, but most of them had left for their homes in other states when the lockdown was announced. As the facilities reopened, we started calling our employees to start coming back to the warehouse. We had a duty to fulfil the needs of the country at a particularly tough time. To our surprise, almost everyone was willing to step up. The only issue was, the police stations under whose jurisdiction the villages were, were enforcing the lockdown strictly and no one was being allowed to leave their homes. This meant that we had to take the order from the central government and go to the different stations to argue with them or convince them to let us do the right thing. Finally, good sense prevailed everywhere and we got our people to start coming to work after issuing them proper ID cards and establishing certain curfew limits. In the process, we had already lost a week. Since the elected officials and influential folks in the villages had similar concerns as our employees, that is, they did not want people working in the facilities to bring back the contagion to the villages, we set up makeshift sleeping arrangements for all workers at the warehouse, overnight, so that everyone who was tested could also stay at the facility and the warehouse itself would operate as a bio-bubble.

Operations had hardly been on for one day when officials from another department arrived and shut down the facility for violating social distancing guidelines in public places. This was just one facility out of the twenty or so that we operated across the country. There were similar scenes of confusion and disarray everywhere.

Even though things eventually settled down, the uncoordinated way in which the supply chain returned to life also demonstrated the lack of understanding we, and everyone around us, had of the challenges that could arise while supplying services across a massive metropolis every day. It seemed that opening up our facilities was the only way thousands of families in lockdown could get their essentials—but this was, of course, not a point of discussion with the authorities. In almost every case, the local agenda took precedence over our ability to operate for the greater good. Over the years, this scenario has played out in multiple ways across different things we have tried to do.

Building in this environment is chaotic and can be frustrating as well, but it is also where I believe the biggest opportunities lie. Our experience with quick commerce and our exposure to everything related to the operations and supply chain side of things clearly points to a need for innovative business models to thrive and be available to improve the quality of life of our customers. We have only talked about retail and transport so far, but shift the thought to the need to scale up and deliver large-scale healthcare services at all price points. In the future, entry-level workers may have better opportunities either through gig work or because large-scale adoption of gig work has driven up labour costs. Wages could rise to a point where missing a day of work to visit a civil hospital to seek healthcare will become too expensive in terms of lost income, encouraging workers to turn to private alternatives to save time and fit-in with their earnings. New businesses may emerge in this space that tie into the way our cities are structured. If there is no dramatic improvement in the commute times or access to different parts of the cities, we should expect innovations in healthcare delivery that are not dependent on large-scale physical infrastructure.

The solutions that are finding prevalence within our cities are outcomes of the environment people find themselves in. The quality of our human capital is going to be dependent on whether our cities and our businesses find the right solutions.

What creates opportunity for private enterprises is poor structure of the process that determines the development of our cities and their upkeep. For instance, in my home city of Gurgaon, we have been actively observing the Maruti Kunj area for the last seven years. According to our estimates, the population density, that is, the actual active population of the locality, and the amount of commercial and residential activity in the area has been the highest in Gurgaon in that period. While to most of us Gurgaon seems to be about Golf Course Road with its multi-crore-rupee apartments, the fact is that the real story of Gurgaon is playing out in Maruti Kunj.

The population of this area alone has likely grown to be the same as the rest of Gurgaon over the last ten years. Not only that, most of the housing in the area isn't part of any city masterplan and, if I were to guess, most housing there exists without documentation.[7] It is now too late to even think about getting into figuring out whether housing there is indeed legal. Schools have come up and ecosystems have been set up for commercial ventures. Maruti Kunj is a thriving city in its own right. It still doesn't have organized drainage or consistent water and electricity supply. It is primarily inhabited by low-income wage earners who have figured out their own micro-economies to survive. The lack of accessible healthcare has led to the sprouting up of some mini dispensaries run by people with questionable medical backgrounds. Institutions for primary education are limited and the quality of both the infrastructure of the schools and those employed in them is questionable. There is no public transport or organized access to public facilities. For the longest time, we looked at the area's growth and weren't sure whether we should serve it as a business. There did not seem to be an economic opportunity for us. Finally, in 2022, we opened our first store in the area. It did 1,000 orders in a single day within the first week, registering one of the fastest scale-ups across the country.

Clearly, the development of areas like Maruti Kunj is what we should be encouraging and planning, but the fact that it is not being actively undertaken and we are reactive to its development means that something is amiss. Even if there is a profit opportunity here, the web of regulations and the fear of local government agencies is impeding it. This is directly stunting our growth as a knowledge economy. Imagine the increased productivity in the workforce if Maruti Kunj had four good schools instead of one, organized healthcare and public transport. The people there have already shown that they are willing to adopt new solutions if these make life better for them: our store's success in that area is proof of that. I believe there will be opportunities for multiple more businesses in a similar vein should they decide to enter. The age-old adage that certain solutions are 'not needed in a low-income society' should be set aside. Maybe it is my naïve, wide-eyed optimism, but I believe that great solutions will emerge if we allow them to. We are seeing the results of doing things the way they have always been done, which are unfortunately inadequate. It is time to think differently about developing our cities and recognize the chain reaction of better outcomes—especially in the productivity of our human capital. Just as India became the global epicentre of quick commerce over the last four years, it could also become a leader in solving urban development problems. Maybe the world's largest urban healthcare, waste management or mass transit start-up will emerge from here.

Our cities will have to become responsive and modern, with unprecedented adoption of technological advancement, if we are to invest in the human capital and the demographic dividend on the back of which we want the country to grow. Any other answer will lead, at best, to a mediocre outcome for all of us while running a high risk of outright failure. I think it is a pipe dream to hope that we will somehow reverse the urban sprawl that has resulted from the unorganized development of our cities. It is much more reasonable to expect that new solutions will be invented to improve the lives of the citizens. I am sure they will lead to plenty of opportunities to build valuable products and services, just like they did for us.

While we were trying to deal with the challenges of building in cities marred by sub-par infrastructure that impacted both our business and people, the same problems started presenting themselves as opportunities for us in our silently blooming dark store business. As we entered 2023, though, the fate of Blinkit changed dramatically. We had agreed to a merger with Zomato (the company would later be renamed Eternal) which would give us the capital to continue building our vision of quick commerce for the long term. What we needed to do now was put our learnings from the previous nine years together and prove that, as an organization, we could make this model work both operationally and financially.

2023

THE NECESSARY TYRANNY OF NOISE

Early in 2023, Akshant Goyal and I were sitting in the conference room of the Mumbai office of one of the biggest public market investors in India. A few months prior to this, Zomato had announced the acquisition of Blinkit in an all-stock deal. As a result, Zomato's share price, which used to be ₹145 when we had agreed on the deal, had tanked to a mere ₹42. A number of Zomato's major shareholders were uneasy about the Blinkit business model. Blinkit was a loss-making business and the execution of the Grofers business prior to changing its name to Blinkit had been patchy. Akshant, the chief financial officer of Zomato, had arranged the meeting so I could respond to questions about the quick commerce space and explain why I was still bullish on the Blinkit business despite spending over nine years building a different one.

However, I didn't get a chance to say much. The investors were very adamant that Zomato divest the Blinkit business. In their view, Zomato's share price would increase if they just got rid of the Blinkit business. It was an uncomfortable conversation, for Akshant most of all, as I was sitting in the room, listening to the company I had built being talked about as an albatross around the neck of a perfectly good business. While the back and forth went on for a while, the meeting ended with me sharing our company's view on why we thought the business would succeed. I do not think I made much of an impression, though. After we left the meeting, Akshant expressed his concern over how the exchange had affected my enthusiasm for building the business. I was clear that the investors' apprehensions would either prove to be right or wrong. We couldn't do anything about their opinions—all we could do was focus on building the business. If we succeeded, then they would be wrong; if we failed, then they would be right. There was nothing personal to take away from the discussion.

This stoic state was relatively new for me. I had endured enough good and bad news, very publicly, over the years and had been emotionally impacted by what was written about the company on social media and in the news. The noise had been constant and witheringly negative for quite a few years—not to mention that sometimes a lot of it felt mean and personal. There was cynicism at every step and a thumping indignation whenever something went wrong. Take the case of the outrage when we were launching deliveries in ten minutes. Social media went into overdrive, questioning the need for grocery deliveries being done in ten minutes, and before we knew it, the narrative had become about rider safety. Most were of the view that we were forcing our drivers to drive fast, because that was how 10-minute delivery would be possible. In a bizarre incident in Lucknow, one of our customers started lecturing the delivery partner on the job to not drive fast as the partner had made the delivery within a few minutes, earlier than was promised. After listening to the customer rant for a few minutes, the delivery partner patiently told them that they had in fact walked from the store which was only 100 metres away from where the customer lived. Eventually, I had to put out a statement to try and explain why the vitriol and anger at the quick-delivery model was misdirected. It hardly made a dent in the sentiment at the time. In fact, even today, despite all the knowledge out there about how the segment functions, the general narrative tends to follow this negativity.

But why is there so much noise? Over the years I have interacted frequently with founders who built businesses in the West and in China, and everyone has some story about how their peace was disturbed by an incident and, at times, by the public discourse that followed. However, nowhere in these ecosystems did the noise seem as consistent and the involved companies as consistently in focus from the get-go as in the Indian ecosystem. Initially, I used to think that it was just my heightened sensitivity to news stories about start-ups in general and our company in particular that made it seem like there was too much noise about it. However, I realized soon enough that there had been an inordinate amount of focus on the start-up sector in India over the last ten years—much more, in fact, than it perhaps merited. As a percentage of the overall Gross Domestic Product (GDP) the contribution of the start-up sector has been much smaller than others and almost negligible—but media coverage and attention on it in general has been higher, and the sector is being even more heavily scrutinized and talked about as starting up, entrepreneurship and fundraising enter the mainstream with the popularity of entrepreneurship-focused reality TV shows.

This coverage has led to an abundance of opinions about early-stage companies, especially in the echo chambers of social media where consumers are quick to point out the good and bad of start-ups. Having been a part of the sector and observing it closely,

I feel there are three primary reasons for this disproportionate focus on the start-up sector in India.

First, the act of building a business has not been a part of mainstream consciousness. Although there were large business houses that had operated for years and smaller businesses that started locally and scaled, at no point in our journey over the first fifty years after Independence did we have narratives that highlighted the merit and opportunity of starting a business in India. In fact, there was a widespread mistrust of businesses. For several businesses that had been built over the last fifty years, the challenges had been everything from trying to function during the License Raj to dealing with a plutocratic environment. That, coupled with a distrust of private businesses in general, was the cultural norm. (Amitabh Bachchan wasn't glamourizing entrepreneurship in the '70s, but was making a hero out of the socialist worker crusader. The 'seth' wasn't an entrepreneur but a greedy exploiter. I still have mixed feelings while watching *Hum*. I feel the character played by Danny Denzongpa, a legend in his own right, got the short end of the stick. For more such portrayals, one can watch *Deewar*, *Coolie* and other similar films.) Several generations were shaped by a healthy suspicion of private businesses, especially large ones, which were viewed as exploitative machines—a sentiment that probably still rings true for the majority of the country. In fact, until businesses like Infosys shone a light on ESOPs and wealth creation, people viewed large businesses as the domain of the elites. Throughout my youth I encountered the notion that if someone was able to deal with the red tape and corruption involved in running a business, then they must also be complicit in it. Whenever a scandal related to any business broke out, it only served to reinforce that narrative.

The rags-to-riches stories of those who founded and ran successful businesses in America, which are so mythologized in

Americana, go back a hundred years. The well-documented rise of the Rockefellers and Zuckerbergs had always highlighted that America was the land of opportunity where meritocracy thrived. I don't remember any of those stories being a part of our general consciousness while I was growing up. In fact, daily political discourse has consistently been the major storyline. A lot of my generation believed that building a career in politics, in order to gain influence instead of serving the public, was the height of achievement. This was also sadly reflected in the career choices of many people who grew up around me.

With no common mythology around businesses, how they are built and what it takes to keep them ticking are not widely understood phenomena. This will remain the case with a segment of the public and, unfortunately, those averages will never work in the favour of founders. As I see it, for a while at least, people who are building businesses in India will have to deal with being both misunderstood and viewed with suspicion by the majority.

Second, the start-up sector, which started post liberalization, has had a massive impact on the day-to-day lives of people. Think of how you get products, how you move around, how you pay and how you plan your holidays. In lockstep with technology and mobile adoption, the way people live their lives has changed dramatically. While the first wave of liberalization brought forth the outsourcing economy and its growth impacted people's aspirations and career choices, the consumer tech ecosystem that bloomed 2007 onwards truly affected people's lives. The consumer tech companies built during this phase made people sit up and take notice, share their experiences and even become more curious about what happens behind the scenes. Whether we like it or not, the frequent touchpoints of consumer start-ups mean that we end up building very publicly. The victories and the missteps, therefore, seem much bigger than they are. Whenever our services have been disrupted, queries from concerned customers and the media have flooded us almost immediately. Similarly, hardships faced by start-ups, whether related to operations, raising capital or lay-offs actioned under duress also get immediate coverage because most of the companies have managed to become household names in a relatively short time.

As I mentioned earlier, this has had a positive impact on the ability of companies to hire, retain and train the talent needed to build great companies in India from scratch. The noise and the hype around the technology and consumer start-up ecosystem have normalized both starting up and working at a start-up a lot more than was the case in 2014.

Lastly, while the hype around start-ups has encouraged the evolution of 'good' companies, it has also attracted ethically questionable entities. For a nascent and growing ecosystem like India's, there are too many start-ups that have been caught in scandals of their own creation—whether arising from dodgy accounting, stretched truths or unkept promises. This is the part of the ecosystem where a new order that is meant to thrive on meritocracy meets an environment in which adherence to the rule of law is fuzzy and the ability to bend rules a little is not necessarily considered unethical—to the point that businesses siphoning off money from their balance sheets is a generally accepted fact.

In 2015, in the period during which we were rapidly expanding our service and getting more orders from our consumer app, we made the decision to shut down our B2B operation—the original one of delivering orders for local businesses. Although it was a nicely profitable small business, we could see that the consumer business could be much larger and we needed to invest all our resources in making that successful. We communicated this news to most of the shops, but I wanted to visit one shop in particular—

one of the first stores I had ever signed up—and thank them in person for giving us our start. The proprietor of the shop was a hard negotiator but he had seen the value in our business model and become the first to sign up for our services. In fact, many of the changes we made in the early days of the business were a direct result of feedback from him. I considered him to be a sharp business operator who had a thriving multi-outlet business. As I sat in his shop and drank the excessively milky tea they served, we talked about the future of Grofers. He was obviously not happy that we were shutting the services as there was no real alternative for him in the market and he would have to resort to hiring and managing delivery personnel on his own. However, he strongly urged me not to abandon a profitable business in the hope of building a larger business that wasn't guaranteed to be profitable.

As he explained, the prudent way of doing business in India is taking money off the table as soon as you can. Most businesses had a deep mistrust of the authorities, the government and the general ecosystem. Even he had been taken for a ride one too many times with proposals of investment, or had been affected by arbitrary changes made in the laws related to his business—so much so that he no longer felt comfortable with capital at risk. A lot of the compliances and rules that he was subject to were, in his view, impractical to follow even when he was running a small business. Businesses like his sometimes borrowed money from the bank, but the owners kept most of it aside for themselves and their families before utilizing some of the cash for the actual business, even if this was unethical. Siphoning money out of businesses or operating them outside the gambit of taxation was unfortunately the norm, and still is, especially in the informal sector.

This was, and still is, the harsh reality for people who believe doing business in India is a mug's game. I did not share this view at the time and still don't, but I understand why so many business owners thought that way. An unfortunate side effect of this is that the ethical boundaries are not really clear to many people who do business. Clean financials and adhering to the law of the land are not priorities for many small businesses.

If you accept that for some people, building this way, with lower integrity, is the norm, and marry it to widespread media coverage of the start-up ecosystem and a venture-backed fundraising environment that only invests in good storytellers in their early days, you have an almost-perfect mix that will attract people who might not have the best intentions. When the venture business is about high risk—high reward, then you will find that great storytellers who are able to overstate the potential rewards are frequent winners. Not all of them have the ethics to build businesses that live up to the promised outcomes. Over the years, as venture-capital investing increased, so did the number of people selling big dreams. In a way, bust cycles are the venture ecosystem's way of tidying up these players every few years. If the failures end up being spectacular, then the noise around them feeds more negative narratives to the public and the cycle continues.

At the end of the day, I still believe the Indian ecosystem is generally super competitive and a certain meritocracy still shows up over the long term. There are a large number of people working on similar ideas and you are not only competing against your direct competitors, but also many other players in smaller segments of the space—for instance, the largest e-commerce companies in India are also competing against last-mile logistics players here. The great thing about building a business like ours was the ability to see how we, and many other companies, had to fight for an edge in so many different spheres, whether it was the lack of access to basic infrastructure services, lopsided regulation, a paucity of capital, or the consumers' preference for products and services. Building something people wanted was never a straightforward goalpost.

In light of these factors, the noise that surrounds the entire ecosystem is, in my view, an essential distraction. Builders have to learn how to cope with it. They need to understand that with the gradual acceptability of start-ups, this noise will bring into the space bigger talent pools, potentially higher investments and the disruption of the established status quo. The bad actors are just another version of the pigeon poop problem that will become irrelevant over time as more builders find success.

2024

BUILDING BLINKIT

I was interviewing a candidate for a growth role with us. My first question while talking to potential team members is always why they want to join us and not any other organization. Her answer was as disarming as it was honest. She said, 'Because Blinkit matters.'

She was a mother of two children with a full-time job. In her own words, for her and her family, Blinkit was the biggest lifestyle upgrade they had made in the last few years. The roads had become more congested, the air was dustier and more polluted, and the weather more unpredictable—but Blinkit had suddenly taken away a large part of the everyday stresses of their lives. She was now ordering gifts when she was taking her kids for a birthday party, snacks when she had guests over, sanitary napkins when she needed them, and much more. She would check on Blinkit every time she needed something urgently. She wanted to work with us because Blinkit came across as a business that needed to be built so more people could access its services.

In one quick moment, someone's simple articulation of what we were doing gave me insight into what it meant to build a company. As an organization, we had started out intending to build a viable commercial venture in which we could use our technological skills. Over time, as we began to understand our consumers and what we needed to do, we started talking more about retailing and the products that our customers needed. Then came the arc of providing value to the customers as that was hard for them to find and, subsequently, we ended up inventing the systems that would power the country's most expansive 10-minute delivery service. While we were improving the way people bought products, we didn't really imagine that what we were doing could potentially reshape the way that people lived their lives. Our journey of ten years had brought us to a point where we needed to think of our business as a tool that people could use to make their lives better. That tool no longer needed to be tied to selling just products.

Technology has reshaped the way the world functions in much the same way as other powerful tools have done for our civilization. From discovering and harnessing fire to utilizing the wheel, human beings have used the tools they discovered or developed to fundamentally reshape how they lived. Whether it was fossil fuels to power our civilization, or internet connectivity to reshape our world view, disruptive opportunities and consequences have always followed the development of high-impact technology.

In the retail sector alone, companies like Walmart were the first to harness the power of computing to run more efficient centralized supply chains—a phenomenon that had been coming for a while, but only truly arrived when a company from rural America fully understood how to add computers to the mix. Their customers no longer had to choose between better prices, quality of products, standardization and range. Due to the presence of a platform like Walmart, consumers reshaped their behaviour and began to drive a few minutes outside of town every week to buy products in bulk. This fundamentally altered American retail supply chains as the search for cheaper alternatives and a reliable supply chain backbone, which was copied quickly, opened the avenue for mass production in China for the American customer.

Similarly, Amazon latched on to the internet to build a company that not only reshaped how supply chains function but changed the expectations of the consumers. You no longer had to limit yourself to the items available in your vicinity; you could pretty much get anything under the sun from anywhere. A company like Uber showed the world that mobile connectivity and smartphones could change the nature of commuting forever. As we apply this multi-dimensional lattice of developments in technology to the needs of a developing country, it is fairly clear that the future is not going to be more of the same.

Customers will use the tools that the world has put in their hands to fundamentally change their lives for the better. A mother of two will not sacrifice her career to run the household if the services she needs arrive at her doorstep; she will never have to choose between career and caregiving. The belief systems prevalent in society, usually the last bastion of dogma, will be challenged. The lack of infrastructure and the substandard quality of life in large cities will be bypassed as more people adopt alternative employment and shun sub-par services in markets to avail at-home services instead. This will create pressure on local commercial hubs to adapt to a different need, which, in turn, will affect the expectations of business and industry from local governments. The private sector will seek a larger role in the quality of life of the citizens in a particular city as more of their businesses get impacted by the outcomes of local development. Governing municipalities will be accountable for the quality of life of citizens and judged on their ability to provide an environment where world-class services are delivered. Today, a middle-income household in Mumbai, or for that matter any Indian city, is fully aware of the services that are available to a family in a different country. Not only do they aspire to live that way, but they actively seek the answer to the question: Why do we not have it?

A powerful idea, when placed in the hands of the customer, reshapes the world they live in. The facility to talk to each other over the phone, over long distances, has made us comfortable with living away from our families. Similarly, the presence of air travel has globalized the world and made it smaller. Now, imagine something as powerful as the convenience of getting anything you want within minutes. How will that reshape the world?

In 2016, when we were going through a bad time and a crisis of confidence, one of our investors, Abheek Anand, had made a strong statement which has stuck with me through the years: *Good product–market fit, bad founders: product–market fit wins. Bad product–market fit, great founders: product–market fit wins.* In a nutshell, if you build something that people want, it can overcome much of what could hold you back. I believe we walked into a world where building Blinkit was not just about building something that people wanted—it was about building something that truly mattered to people.

Through the journey of building Blinkit, I have experienced many flavours of emotion—pain, elation, sorrow, joy, humiliation, humility. But the one that I wish to hold on to has been the wonder of building something that is a part of so many people's lives—our employees, gig workers and customers. Each day, the objective of making Blinkit mean a little more to everyone involved has been the underlying force driving me.

In addition to the operating lessons of building a business in India that I have described in the pages preceding this one, there are a few things that I have learnt mostly because everyone around me has allowed me the privilege to observe and comment while they acted ceaselessly to keep the business running, growing and thriving.

There are no decisive victories and no decisive losses.

Certain chapters end, sure. As a somewhat older man today, I can perhaps say that I won in the arena of business the day I stepped out and decided to start this company with SK. We won when we received our first revenue cheque from a store. We won the day Rishi decided to join us. He was the first person we shared our dream with and who truly believed in it. We won again when we received our first cheque from Deepi and Sequoia Capital, our first investors.

Alongside, we saw losses galore. We lost the day we got our first rejection while fundraising. We lost the first time we had to lay off people from the company in 2016. We lost when we had to fold the 90-minute delivery model and move to next-day delivery. We lost the day we shut down the next-day delivery model.

The wins and losses were not as linear as the timelines suggest, though. They were more like a rotating carousel where the wins led to losses and debilitating losses became victories in subsequent moments. It is inhuman to expect the people involved in the business to not be emotional about these moments and we never expected that of ourselves. Setbacks hurt, being low brings you down, sometimes beyond help. However, the joy you feel also never reaches escape velocity. There is gravity in business. The joy comes from the life you build for yourself while all of this is unfolding.

Smiles around you matter.

Thousands of people allowed me to build this company with them and that matters more to me than anything else. On many days, I felt irritated and demotivated, but for the most part I only remember smiling, helpful faces. I don't remember a single person who let me down or whom I was unhappy with—if Blinkit was a person it would be this hybrid smiling person made of the faces of the thousands who have been here and who helped build the company. People who let me take credit for everything they have done. If anyone reading this book ever decides to build a company, it will help them to remember that doing it with folks who make you happy on most days matters—just like choosing a life partner.

There is no one way.

This has been said to death, but I will repeat it. Companies get built in many different ways. However, they never get built if the founder is not being themself. The journey of who you are as a person is a lifelong process and at some point it might intersect with your journey as a founder, when one will shape the other. At no point, though, can the journey unfold behind a veneer of falsity. The founders of companies, the people who build them, those that back them, the customers who support them—they all create a unique thumbprint for what each company's culture, ethos, drive and impact looks like. You have to be willing to accept and live with the lasting imprint of what you have built on the world. Chances are, if it is a meaningful endeavour, that thumbprint of what you have built is going to be the only thing that will be remembered.

Blinkit turned profitable for the first time in March 2024. The business has since become one of the most well-known retailers in India. I still love going to work every day.

Thank you for reading *Buildit*. All proceeds from this book will go to the ACAD Foundation, run by my wife, Akriti and me, to support initiatives in working-class neighbourhoods that are focused on primary education, healthcare and the enhancement of local infrastructure by working with municipal governments.

ACKNOWLEDGEMENTS

This book is the story of my journey building Blinkit and the lessons I learnt along the way. To everyone who played a part—supporting Blinkit and cheering it on—*Buildit* is dedicated to you. Thank you for letting me live a dream with your contribution and optimism.

Buildit is a result of the direct effort of several people, including Akriti, Vivek Choudhary, Mansi Srivastava, Poulomi Chatterjee and Rachel Rojy, and the entire team at HarperCollins India. Thank you for your feedback and hard work in bringing this book to life and sharing it with the world.

Ultimately, I need to acknowledge the wonderfully diverse customers and people of India who make building here both a challenge and a delight. Thank you.

NOTES

A Journey of Two Decades

1. Current Minimum Wage Rate. Order No. F.No.12 (142)/02/MW/VII/5063. Government of NCT of Delhi (Labour Department).

2014: Trust at the Bottom of the Pyramid

1. Assuming two repairs per year, the average cost for motorbike repairs was approximately Rs 600.
   National Sample Survey Office. (2016). 'Key Indicators of Household Expenditure on Services and Durable Goods'. NSS 72nd Round.
2. Press Trust of India. (2022). 'Of 220 Million Applicants, over 722,000 Got Govt Jobs in 2014–22: Centre'. *Business Standard.*
3. Edelman Trust Institute. (2025). 'Edelman Trust Barometer: 2015–2025'.
4. National Sample Survey Office. (2013). 'Key Indicators of Household Consumer Expenditure in India'. NSS 68th Round.
5. Adhvaryu et al. (2021). 'Dealing with Worker Absenteeism in Labour-Intensive Industries'. International Growth Centre.
6. Edelman Trust Institute. (2025). 'Edelman Trust Barometer: 2015–2025'.
7. National Sample Survey Office. (2014). 'Education in India'. NSS 71st Round.

8. International Labour Organization. (2024). 'India Employment Report 2024: Youth Employment, Education and Skills'.
9. World Bank. (2019). 'The World Development Report 2019: The Changing Nature of Work'.
10. Zomato. (2025). 'Shareholders' Letter and Results: Q3FY25'.
11. Wallenstein, J., de Chalendar, A., Reeves, M. and Bailey, A. (2019). 'The New Freelancers: Tapping Talent in the Gig Economy'. Boston Consulting Group.
12. Augustinraj, R., Jain, V., and Bansal, S. (2021). 'Unlocking the Potential of the Gig Economy in India'. Boston Consulting Group and Michael & Susan Dell Foundation.
13. Ibid.
14. Ibid.

2015: Gambling and Capital

1. Nielsen. (2016). 'Global Connected Commerce: Consumer Purchasing in Today's Digital Economy'.
2. Reserve Bank of India. (2015). 'Reserve Bank of India Annual Report 2014–25'.
3. KPMG and CII. (2015). 'The New Wave Indian MSME: An Action Agenda for Growth'.
4. Reserve Bank of India. (2024). 'India Non Performing Loans Ratio 1998–2024.' CEIC Data.
5. Gautam, V. (2022). 'At Rs 2.4 Lakh Crore, Willful Loan Defaults in India Are Higher Than 87 Countries' GDP'. Indiatimes.
6. International Finance Corporation. (2018). 'Financing India's MSMEs: Estimation of Debt Requirement of MSMEs in India'.
7. Annamalai, T. (2015). '2015 India Venture Capital and Private Equity Report: An Analysis of Valuation and Structuring of Venture Investments'.
8. Tracxn. (2025). 'Flipkart Company Profile'.
9. Comscore. (2015). 'The 2015 U.S. Mobile App Report'.
10. Sheth, A., Rajan, S. and Bhaskaran, K. (2016). 'India Private Equity Report 2016'. Bain & Co.

2016: Pigeon Poop Problems

1. Rajagopalan, S. and Tabarrok, A.T. (2014). 'Lessons from Gurgaon, India's Private City'. in: David Emanuel Andersson & Stefano Moroni (ed.), *Cities and Private Planning*, chapter 10, pp. 199–231, Edward Elgar Publishing.
2. Poushter, J. (2016). 'Smartphone Ownership and Internet Usage Continues to Climb in Emerging Economies'. Pew Research Center.
3. National Sample Survey Office. (2024). 'Comprehensive Annual Modular Survey, 2022-23'. NSS 79th Round.

2017: The Mind of a Customer

1. PricewaterhouseCoopers. (2024). 'How India Shops Online: Consumer Preferences in the Metropolises and Tier 1-4 Cities'.
2. NASSCOM. (2021). 'Job Creation and Hiring in Indian IT-BPM Industry'.
3. American Express. (2017). 'American Express 2017 Global Customer Service Barometer'.
4. Mastercard. (2023). 'Ecommerce Fraud Trends and Statistics Merchants Need to Know in 2024'.
5. Internet and Mobile Association of India. (2014). 'Internet in India 2014'.

2018: Working Hard for ESOPs

1. AON. (2016). 'Entering the Era of the "New Normal" in Salary Increases in India'.
2. Ghosh, A. and D'Monte, L. (2024). 'Start-Ups Are the New Hi-tech Job Creators'. Mint.
3. Startup Genome. (2022). 'State of the Global Startup Economy'.
4. Kashyap, K. (2024). 'ESOP Buybacks: 3,000+ Startup Employees Made over INR 1,450 Cr in 2024'. Inc42.

2019: (Re)Building with Community

1. Jha, R. (2024). 'Improving Urban Freight Transport'. Observer Research Foundation.

2. Nizam, A., Sivakumar, P. and Rajan, S. (2022). 'Interstate Migration in India during the COVID-19 Pandemic: An Analysis Based on Mobile Visitor Location Register and Roaming Data'. *Journal of South Asian Development*, 17(3), 271–296.
3. FICCI–Deloitte. (2019). 'Evolve for Consumer'.
4. World Justice Project. (2023). 'Rule of Law Index: 2023 Insights'.

2022: The Opportunity in Our Cities

1. Oxford Economics. (2024). 'Oxford Economics Global Cities Index'.
2. Indian Roads Congress. (2018). 'Geometric Design Standards for Urban Roads in Plains'.
3. Thai, J., Laurent-Brouty, N. and Bayen, A.M. (2016). 'Negative Externalities of GPS-Enabled Routing Applications: A Game Theoretical Approach'. Institute of Electrical and Electronics Engineers.
4. Transportation for America. (2020). 'The Congestion Con: How More Lanes and More Money Equals More Traffic'.
5. NASA. (2022). 'NASA's ECOSTRESS Detects "Heat Islands" in Extreme Indian Heat Wave'.
6. Niti Aayog. (2021). 'Fast Tracking Freight in India: A Roadmap for Clean and Cost-Effective Goods Transport'.
7. Indian Institute of Technology, Roorkee. (2024). 'Population Projections of GMUC and Gual Pahari Urbanisable Residential Areas'.

ABOUT THE AUTHOR

Albinder Singh Dhindsa is the founder of Blinkit, a pioneer in India's quick commerce retailing. Born in Punjab, India, into a farming family, he went on to earn a bachelor's degree in engineering before turning to entrepreneurship. As someone who has benefited from India's economic growth, he is passionate about giving back to the ecosystem, both with learnings and support, to create greater positive economic impact for more people.

HarperCollins *Publishers* India

At HarperCollins India, we believe in telling the best stories and finding the widest readership for our books in every format possible. We started publishing in 1992; a great deal has changed since then, but what has remained constant is the passion with which our authors write their books, the love with which readers receive them, and the sheer joy and excitement that we as publishers feel in being a part of the publishing process.

Over the years, we've had the pleasure of publishing some of the finest writing from the subcontinent and around the world, including several award-winning titles and some of the biggest bestsellers in India's publishing history. But nothing has meant more to us than the fact that millions of people have read the books we published, and that somewhere, a book of ours might have made a difference.

As we look to the future, we go back to that one word—a word which has been a driving force for us all these years.

Read.

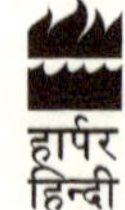

www.ingramcontent.com/pod-product-compliance
Lightning Source LLC
LaVergne TN
LVHW091341110826
845155LV00043B/1
* 9 7 8 9 3 6 9 8 9 9 4 3 2 *